When the Supernatural Becomes Natural

By Joan Pearce

Channel of Love Ministry

Channel of Love Ministries, Intl.
Joan and Marty Pearce
www.joanpearce.org

ISBN 978-1987486131

All Scripture quotations are taken from The Holy Bible, **New King James Version** Copyright © 1982 by Thomas Nelson, Inc. Used by permission. All rights reserved.

Cover design by Jim Art.

Dedication Page

I would like first of all to thank my Lord and Savior Jesus Christ for saving my soul and writing my name in the Lamb's Book of Life. Without the leading of the Holy Spirit this book would not have come about. For it is written, "'Not by might nor by power, but by My Spirit,' says the Lord of hosts." (Zechariah 4:6) I give all praise to the Lord Almighty for leading me and guiding me in writing this book according to His will. Amen!

A personal thanks to my beloved husband Marty and to my children: Alan, Rob and Carrie, for their encouragement to me. I also want to thank God for bringing Godly servants to me and giving them the gift of Wisdom. (1 Corinthians 12:8)

A very special thanks to Anton Wellbrock for his countless hours of work on this book, and to Pat McLaughlin for editing.

Thank you to Jim and Robin Art for your hours of creative work on the design of the book cover. There are so many other beautiful saints that were a blessing to me. There isn't enough paper in this book to thank them all by name. A sincere thanks to each and every one of you. May God richly bless you!

Joan Peace

Table of Contents

INTRODUCTION

God has burned down deep inside of me an urgency to write *When the Supernatural Becomes Natural.*

This book has literally been burned into my heart and soul day and night for over a period of many years.

God said, Prepare My People for what is coming upon the world, so they can be ready.

FIRST WE MUST SEE AND RECOGNIZE THE TRUTH.

The Truth is that the fate of the entire world is at stake! Jesus said He IS the Way, the Truth and the Life.

Jesus has left all of us, God's children, here on earth to be His hands, His feet, His voice. We need to go forth into this world with the Truth about Jesus' Life, Death, Burial and Resurrection!

JESUS HAS ENTRUSTED US WITH THIS WORLD'S ONLY ANSWERS. JESUS!

Your life and your loved one's lives depend on you hearing God and living in the Supernatural. This is not only for your family.

There are People crying out right now: "Somebody help Me!" This may even be You!

Many people don't know how to make it from day to day. Marriages are falling apart. Children of all ages are: running away, getting hurt, being abused, getting on drugs, being used for sex trade. The list goes on and on.

It is crisis after crisis. People are living in fear.

Open your eyes and your heart. See the real condition of this world. Know we are truly living in the Last Days.

IT IS CRUCIAL THAT YOU LIVE IN THE SUPERNATURAL OR YOU WON'T MAKE IT THROUGH THESE TRYING TIMES. God wants to use His Church [All of Us] to be ready for the greatest harvest of souls.

God wants us to step out in the Power of God and live in the Supernatural.

This book has been designed to teach you, equip you, and motivate you.

The beginning chapter lays down foundational principles and precepts.

As you read on, you will find things which demonstrate how you can go forth in the natural world you are presently living in and live in the Supernatural.

You will find teachings which will help you clarify what you are to do, plus encouraging stories which are living illustrations.

GOD WILL USE YOU TO WALK
IN THE SUPERNATURAL.

CHAPTER 1
Walking in God's Glory

This book is all about us walking in the Supernatural. God wants us to live in the Supernatural. When we received Jesus as our Savior, we became children of God.

God's Word says, "Thy Kingdom come, Thy will be done on earth as it is in Heaven." WE ARE IN GOD'S KINGDOM.

All human beings will live forever and ever because we are eternal beings.

There are two forces working on this earth. There is God, and angels; there is Satan and demons, which are fallen angels.

We have choices while we are living here on earth. You can choose God, by following Jesus or you can follow Satan. The choice you make here is what determines where you will spend eternity, in heaven or in hell.

The stakes are so high here regarding the choices we are all given! It is absolutely crucial that we believers share the Good News of the Gospel of Jesus Christ. What a horrible thought to think of anyone having to live forever and ever in Hell!

❧ Man is a Supernatural Being ❧

We need to walk in the Supernatural with God's Power and Authority so we can be led by the Spirit and share Jesus.

As we traveled all over the United States and the world, many people have excitedly come up to share their supernatural experiences with us. What amazes us so often is that the experiences they share happened to them a year ago, or months ago. These supernatural encounters are few and far between.

This should not be the case! As you continue to learn more about the Supernatural and how to walk in it, the Supernatural will become natural for you. It will become an every-day occurrence. You will be amazed at how God is miraculously using you.

As I shared earlier it is important to know and consider some essential precepts and principles.

This is based on

1 Thessalonians 5:23

Now may the God of peace himself sanctify you completely.. .and may your whole Spirit, Soul and Body be presented blameless at the coming of our Lord Jesus Christ.

All human beings are 3-part beings: SPIRIT, SOUL AND BODY, whether they ever know or recognize this or not.

SPIRIT. The spirit part of us is in the invisible Supernatural Realm. God desires that the Spirit part be what determines everything we are and do.

A Biblical Picture of Man

Man – A Three-Part Whole
(I Thessalonians 5:23)

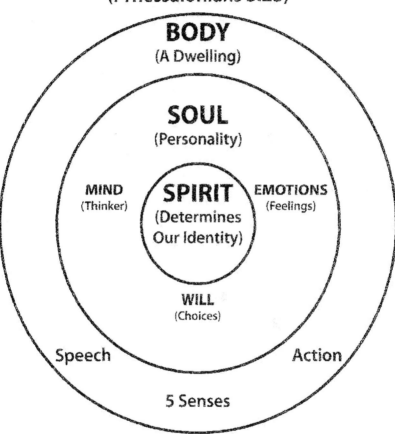

BODY
(A Dwelling)

SOUL
(Personality)

MIND
(Thinker)

SPIRIT
(Determines
Our Identity)

EMOTIONS
(Feelings)

WILL
(Choices)

Speech

Action

5 Senses

SOUL. This is our mind, our will and our emotions. It determines how we will act and how we will mentally think and make choices.

THE BODY. This is the shell we live in while we are here on planet earth. This part of us is governed by our SOUL. It will act based on what we sense, desire and think.

Your thinking must be based on God's thinking.

Romans 12:1,2

I beseech you therefore, brethren, by the mercies of God, that you present your bodies a living sacrifice, holy, acceptable to God, which is your reasonable service. And do not be conformed to this world, but be transformed by the renewing of your mind that you may prove what is good and acceptable and the perfect will of God.

When we start thinking right and let the Holy Spirit lead us, we want to be good and kind and do what is right. Then the world will be a better place.

1 Thessalonians 5:16-18

Rejoice! Pray without ceasing. In everything give thanks for this is the will of God in Christ Jesus for you.

1 Thessalonians 5:24

He who calls you is faithful, who also will do it.

❧ In the Beginning ☙

Go in your Bibles to Genesis 3. Let's go right back to the beginning and read

Genesis 3:4,5

Then the serpent said to the woman, 'You will not surely die for God knows that in the day that you eat of it, your eyes will be opened and you will be like God, knowing good and evil.'

The devil is constantly doing the same thing: deceiving God's people.

The body of Christ needs to be in the Word more. It surprises me how many Christians just fall into things. There are people who say, "Give a thousand dollars and I'll give you a prophecy." Do you have to pay for a prophecy? No.

When we know the word of God or when they say, "Jesus is coming on such and such day." We should know the word of God and be so in tune with the Word of God that we are not deceived by the serpent. They were deceived by the serpent. "Come on, eat this fruit. If you do, you'll be like God." The truth is that they became like Satan. That's the truth.

They were cast out of the Garden and sin came into the world because of it.

Genesis 3:6

Then the woman saw that the tree was good for food and it was pleasant to the eye. The tree was desirable to make one wise. She took of the fruit and ate it. She also gave to her husband with her, and he ate.

Isn't that how Satan works now? He tries to entice us and make sin look good. If something looks bad, you're not going to want to eat it. If it looks terrible you're not going to want it. But he entices us. Satan is still using the same approaches he did with Adam and Eve in the Garden.

If we're going to walk in the Supernatural we need to be aware of the wiles of the devil and how he tries to discourage us.

Genesis 3:6-11

She also gave to her husband and her husband ate. Then their eyes were both opened. They knew that they were naked so they sewed fig leaves together to make themselves covering. And they heard the sound of the Lord God walking in the garden in the cool of the day. Adam and his wife hid themselves from the presence of the Lord God among the trees of the garden.

Then the lord called to Adam and said to him,
'Where are you?'
So he said, 'I hear your voice in the garden and I
was afraid because I was naked and hid myself.'
He said, 'Who told you that you were naked?
Have you eaten from the tree of which I
commanded you that you should not eat?'

We have no idea how long Adam was with God in the Garden after God blew the breath of life into him. Adam had dominion over everything God created. That's what God wants. God wants you and me to know we have dominion over everything in this Earth because of Jesus.

But sin will separate us from walking in the Supernatural. If you're living in sin and trying to walk in the Supernatural, it just won't happen. When you're trying to cast the devil out of someone, the devil will look at you, laugh and say, "I'm not coming out because you're a phony."

What I'm saying is, when Adam and Eve opened themselves up to sin, they fell into the trap of the devil. Thus they knew they were naked. But how long did Adam have fellowship every morning with God Almighty? Can you imagine that? Can you imagine the glory of being able to see God Almighty face to face and live?

We will see God when we all go to heaven. But we'll have a new, glorified body. How many years was Adam in the Garden before God said, "It's not good for man to be alone"? Then he created a woman from his rib. How long were Adam and Eve in the

Garden enjoying fellowship with God every day which is what God wanted and still wants?

God wants us to walk in glory. He wants us to walk in the Supernatural. Adam and Eve were already supernatural beings made in the image of God when they fell into the trap of Satan.

They knew they were naked because they had been clothed with a robe of glory. When God placed them in the Garden and they had been filled with His glory, His anointing and His power and His glory was on them. The truth of the matter is they were physically naked all the time.

But when God's mantle and glory were taken off of them, they knew they were naked.

Katherine Kuhlman, John G. Lake, Smith Wigglesworth and all mightily anointed men and women of God have been able to tap into this real heavy anointing which once was on Adam and Eve, and you can too.

The reason they had this heavy anointing is that they spent hours in fellowship with God. They lived a sacrificial consecrated life filled with prayer and being in the Word.

When Katherine Kuhlman walked through an airport the glory cloud, which was on Adam and Eve at the beginning was so strong on her, that people ten feet on either side would fall under the power of God. There's no limit to the Holy Spirit. The Holy Spirit wants to use you.

We have experienced strong anointings in some of our services.

Every one can walk in this type of anointing. It's God's desire that you walk in the Supernatural. We need to recognize the power and authority which Jesus Christ gave us when he died on the cross.

1 John 3:8

He who sins is of the devil, for the devil has sinned from the beginning. For this purpose the Son of God was manifested, that He might destroy the works of the devil.

Colossians 3:1-4

If then you were raised with Christ, seek those things which are above, where Christ is, sitting at the right hand of God. Set your mind on things above, not on things on the earth. For you died, and your life is hidden with Christ in God. When Christ who is our life appears, then you also will appear with Him in glory.

You can then walk in the same glory. You have been translated from the kingdom of Satan to the Kingdom of God.

We were just like Adam and Eve – kicked out and weren't accepted anymore. Because of sin, we have to be reconnected and be accepted. Blessed be God who has blessed us with every spiritual blessing. Through the blood and the cross of Calvary, we are now reconnected. It's called new birth, being born again. We're reconnected so that we can walk from glory to glory.

We can walk with heavenly power when we stay in the presence of God and we let God's anointing power flow through us. One person can change a city.

One person can impact a nation. When John G. Lake was in South Africa during the Bubonic plague, he instructed the doctors to put the disease on his hand. He prayed in tongues in the Holy Ghost. When they looked under the microscope, they could not see the disease; it had disappeared. We have that kind of power. Many Christians are not walking in that realm.

But we can and God's Word says it.

Acts 1:8

But you shall receive power when the Holy Spirit has come upon you; and you shall be witnesses to Me in Jerusalem, and in all Judea and Samaria, and to the end of the earth.

The word power in this Scripture comes from the Greek work *dunimis* and is used in the English word dynamite. That means power to blow up mountains. God has given us this power.

Some churches in America are wimps. There are a few people who have caught on to it and walked in *dunimis* power. They've been world changers: John G. Lake, Smith Wigglesworth, Aimee Semple

McPherson, Katherine Kuhlman and so many more. There are many who have learned how to tap into it.

Do you think they were just special people? Do you think that God has favorite ones? No! God wants to use you and everyone.

Anyone can walk in this realm of the Supernatural. All you have to do is press in. Press in and walk in the manifestation of the glory of God and you will never be the same. God will seal you with the Holy Spirit and Promise and will take you to a new level.

❥ Blizzard in New York ❧

Let me share an awesome visitation we had where God's glory fell. We were having a series of meetings in upstate New York. At that time there was a terrible blizzard but we went ahead and had our services. A bunch of people made the effort to get there. Even the pastor called on the phone and said, "I'm sorry, sister Joan. We live so far away and it's not safe. We're not going to be there."

Only about forty people showed up who lived close to the church. The glory of God fell. I tried to preach and I couldn't preach. I started calling out people. "You over there, come up here. This is the disease you have. Come up here." They came out of their seats and some fell under the power of God right in their seats. They could not even came to the front, they just fell.

I kept telling them to come forward so I could pray for them. But evidently, God didn't need me to pray for them because whenever they came up, as soon as they come past the seat, boom! Boom, they'd go. Even some were crawling on the floor, trying to come forward so I could pray for them.

When I tried to preach, the power of God started knocking me down and I started falling. I grabbed hold of the podium and I'm still trying to preach. But I kept falling. The next thing I know, the piano player stops playing. I looked over to see why she wasn't playing anymore. She'd slid off the bench and she was laid out under the keyboard, out under the power of God. We were all out under the power of God.

We told the pastor about this awesome service. The next night the word got out and everybody made it through the blizzard. Standing room only; wall to wall. The power of God hit again. As I prayed for people they just fell out. We waited for them to get up but they wouldn't move. So we started moving the pews and prayed for line after line until everyone in the church was on the floor. The last two people standing were me and the pastor. He laid hands on me and I laid hands on him and we were on the floor under God's power. We were all on the floor for about 45 minutes. All you could hear were people crying. We truly had a visitation of God's power.

Why? We pressed in. God wants us to walk in this realm.

It's easy to stay home when there's a blizzard. But when you press in God sees your faithfulness. The devil will do everything he can to interrupt and stop people from walking in the Supernatural.

❧ Walking in God's Glory ❧

Exodus 33:11-14

So the Lord spoke to Moses face to face, as a man speaks to his friend. And he would return to the camp, but his servant Joshua the son of Nun, a young man, did not depart from the tabernacle.

Then Moses said to the Lord, "See, You say to me, 'Bring up this people.' But You have not let me know whom You will send with me. Yet You have said, 'I know you by name, and you have also found grace in My sight.' Now therefore, I pray, if I have found grace in Your sight, show me now Your way, that I may know You and that I may find grace in Your sight. And consider that this nation is Your people." And He said, "My Presence will go with you, and I will give you rest."

Isn't what Moses asked God for what we want too? If we are going to walk in the realm of the Supernatural we have to be like Moses. He didn't want to do anything without having the presence of God.

This remains true today. There is nothing we Christians can do unless God's presence goes with us.

But today we Christians are privileged, because of our born again salvation experience. We are able to choose to hunger and thirst for a deeper relationship with God.

1 Corinthians 2:2

For I determined not to know anything among you except Jesus Christ and him crucified.

Matthew 5:6

Blessed are those who hunger and thirst for righteousness, For they shall be filled.

We have to have a hunger in us which wants to walk in a realm which very few people have walked in. John G. Lake and many other mighty men and women had this powerful sense of urgency and mission!

There are so many people we have never heard about who have raised people from the dead, walked on water and have been involved in marvelous miraculous happenings. But God knows them all. God wants you and me to walk in that realm. We need to have the same presence of God that Moses was crying out for.

"I don't want to go anywhere or see anything if God's presence and His anointing are not there." This is what Moses besought God for. When you let the presence of God which is in you flow through you, you will also find yourself in God's rest.

Then he said to Him, "If Your Presence does not go with us, do not bring us up from here. For how then will it be known that Your people and I have found grace in Your sight, except You go with us? So we shall be separate, Your people and I, from all the people who are upon the face of the earth."

God wants us to be separated as His people. We are to live in the world, but not be of the world. Moses is saying, "Don't take us out of where we are right now unless You go with us. We are Your people; we are Your chosen people."

We must also have God's favor. Today we are God's children and we are His hand extended. We are His mouth. We are the ones who must do what God has called us to do. We are to go forth and preach His Gospel with the anointing and the glory of God.

We don't dare go out and preach without the presence of God and His anointing.

The people of today's world are searching for the Supernatural, but mostly in all the wrong places. Why do you think movies, TV programs, video games, toys and all kinds of books (especially books for children) are about witchcraft, psychics, fortune telling, vampires, and all manner of New Age topics?

Why do you think they are looking for and becoming fascinated with this kind of power?

God's Church should be walking in this power. God has given the Church the power to demonstrate the miraculous, supernatural signs and wonders. But this is all being hidden within the four walls of church buildings.

Let's not hide this power anymore! It needs to be demonstrated throughout the world, so the unsaved, the afraid, the lonely, the sick and desperate can clearly see the demonstration of God's great power. God just needs us believers to step out and be used in our Every Day Life in the realm of the Supernatural.

CHAPTER 2
Betty's Persistence!

I was in my twenties working and raising my children. This was before I had received Jesus into my heart. It was then when my neighbor Betty Powell who lived across the street from me was used in the realm of the Supernatural. She was able to lead many people to the Lord who were hard nuts to crack. The Bible says go into the highways and the by-ways and hedges and compel them that they will be saved. This lady, Betty was like a dog on a bone.

She was led to come over to my house at a time when Jehovah Witnesses and people from various other cults were coming to my house. She decided she had to lead me to the saving knowledge of Jesus Christ.

When she came over and started telling me about Jesus, I was not very nice to her. I would blow smoke in her face until her eyes would be watering and the whole kitchen would be full of smoke.

Soon she started buying me Bibles. She said, "Here." She gave me a Bible. She didn't know I didn't know how to read. I was too embarrassed to tell her. I made one excuse after another as to why I hadn't read any of the Bibles she gave me.

Six Bibles later, she asked me if I'd read any of them, and I hadn't.

One time when she came over, I was on drugs. She upset me so badly I told her, "Get the blank-blank out of here! Stop bringing me all those Bibles!"

She went out the front door. I picked up all six Bibles that were sitting on my bookcase near the door. As she was walking across the street, I threw all six Bibles at her and not one of them hit her.

Because of my Catholic upbringing, I was sure a lightning bolt would strike me dead. I thought I better pick up all those Bibles before my children come home from school. I had always taught them to respect books and especially The Holy Bible.

The next day as I'm having my morning coffee, I see Betty walking across the street and I say, "She better not be coming to my house! I'm going to give her a piece of my mind."

When she arrived at my door I was so angry! When I opened the door I startled myself by saying, "Hi, Betty. Come in. Would you like a cup of coffee?" I started being a little nicer, and felt it was time to be honest with her. I explained I hadn't read any of her Bibles because I didn't know how to read.

The very next day she arrives at my door with a set of *The New Testament* on tape plus a new tape recorder. Didn't I mention she was very persistent!

The Bible says faith comes by hearing and hearing by the Word of God.

One day I came home from work and found the Monsignor from the Catholic Church parked in my driveway. I immediately panicked, thinking something must have happened. Why else would he be here like this!

The Monsignor said, "Young lady I want to talk to you. May I come in and have a cup of coffee?" While we were having coffee he said, "I understand you are making plans to leave the Catholic Church."

I responded, "Who told you this?" He said, "Your neighbor Betty called the Church and she said, 'If you don't want to lose a member, you'd better get over right away to her house.'"

The fact is I was getting ready to be baptized in another church, one which was a cult, on that upcoming weekend.

I was so angry at Betty! How dare she call this Priest on me!

The Monsignor explained, "She wants you to go with her to a Catholic Bible Study."

Soon after the Monsignor left, Betty came over. She said, "Did you tell the Priest you would go to a Bible study with me? Well it so happens there is a study going on tonight."

I thought, "How convenient." I wondered if it was a set up. Nonetheless when she said she would you go with me, I said yes.

I drove my own car so I could leave when I wanted to. I met her there.

We both went to the *Full Gospel Businessmen's* meeting. A Catholic minister was preaching at their dinner meeting.

Afterwards, when the meal was over everyone formed a circle and they were praying. Even though I didn't understand what happened, I felt something tingling all through my body. I was feeling the presence of God.

After the preaching, the evangelist was praying for everyone and doing an altar call. Betty said, "Joan, go up to the altar and let him pray for you. I'll go up there with you." I said, "No, Betty, I don't want to even get near that man."

I said the meeting is over now and I am going home. I go out to my car and she is following me. She talks to me saying, "Joan you can't leave." I said, "I am going home now."

Betty knows I am joining a cult in a few days and she is desperate.

She said, "Please Joan, I don't feel well. I feel sick right now." So I'm in my car with the engine running and she is outside the car saying would I please just go back with her long enough so he can pray for her.

We go back into the building. The meeting was in a restaurant. We walk up to the man of God and he prays for her. After he prayed for her he immediately grabs me and starts praying for me.

I say, "I feel sick. I feel like I'm going to throw up." He drags me through the restaurant into the lady's room. He has me over the toilet. He is saying, come out in the Name of Jesus. Come out in the Name of Jesus. All of a sudden I feel something deep inside of me, clawing in me like it really doesn't want to come out.

I think in my head, if he says Jesus one more time I'm going to kill him. Then he said Jesus one more time, and I came charging at him full force to kill him. He said, "In the Name of Jesus come out." I felt the demon come out and I started to fall.

The man of God caught me in his arms. I was crying. I was scared. The man of God said. "Don't be afraid, you're alright now."

Note:

After you have cast the devil out of anybody make sure they have received Jesus as their Savior. After they have been set free, lead them to Christ and the Baptism of the Holy Spirit.

Betty told the man of God I was saved. I had been at some crazy meeting where the people made me pray. She thought I had been saved but I never really meant what I said. Since I didn't really mean it in my heart I was truly not saved.

Now I am headed home from the meeting. I'm going to tell you about how the devil tried to kill me!

❧ Demons Are Real ❧

How did I find out demons are real?

Let me share my encounter with a demon. I left the Full Gospel Men's meeting thinking I was alright, having been both saved and delivered from demons. So I headed out to the parking lot by myself and started the drive home.

Meanwhile, at that other meeting I went to, I had confessed Jesus as my Lord while I was under rebellion. Therefore I was really not saved. So I'm now free of the demon but I am not yet saved.

NOTE THIS.

In the realm of the supernatural there are angels. There are devils. There are demons. So we need to know there is still a whole lot going on in the heavenly realm which we don't understand.

We know that demons are always trying to attack people. As born again believers, we have the power to set people free in the Name of Jesus.

Some people entertain devils and some people don't want to be set free. But if you have the power, as the Evangelist who delivered me had, there is a way to make the devil leave. Devils only leave when commanded to do so in the Name of Jesus and by the Blood of Jesus, the Lamb of God.

It was Jesus who delivered me. So now I am in my car when the supernatural becomes natural. I don't understand the supernatural, but nonetheless it is coming into my natural reality. It is a realm filled with demons, angels, and the devil – a real realm out there.

Now remember how I told you about my neighbor Betty's persistence about getting me saved. She had brought me a New Testament on tapes and a tape recorder because she knew I couldn't read. I had put the recorder with the tape of the book of Matthew on the front seat of the car. It offered me good company as I drove a lot for work.

As a Catholic, I had been taught little about the Bible or the meaning of salvation. So now I'm driving along as a Catholic lady who thinks she has just gotten saved. Plus I've just had some demons cast out of me. And what do I really know about the supernatural realm?

All of a sudden, my car starts driving itself. My steering wheel is actually trying to drive into the embankment and kill me.

The steering wheel has me turning towards this huge cement block. Meanwhile I'm fighting to steer the wheel with every bit of strength I have, pulling it, trying to keep from killing myself. The car is still driving itself. It keeps on sliding on and off the road towards dangerous obstacles. As I continue to yank the wheel to get control, suddenly I look into my rear view mirror and I see a demon. It's actually sitting there.

I hear myself saying, "O my God!" Fear gripped me. It's unlike any normal fear. This fear is just a terrible fear.

HEAR ME:

This demon is a real demon. Awhile later when I was in a store, I saw some toys that kids were buying.

I remember seeing such toys in India and exclaiming, "There it is. That toy looks just like the demon I saw around the time I got saved." A lot of these toys are demons. They can and are capable of brainwashing our children and sometimes even us into thinking demons are cute and fun to play with. They're just playful imps. Movies, video games and many other popular garbage items out there can do this too.

Getting back to my very real demon experience ... I turned back to see if it was still there. It's there alright, and now it's like I'm petrified scared. But I don't know what to do. And the car keeps driving. And the car starts going into the embankment again when I'm getting back on the freeway. I'm scared. And I'm shaking with fear. But, I don't know what to do next.

Remember my background is Catholic and I can't read. I'm just barely learning the Bible through these cassettes. It became so scary in the car.

I pushed the tape recorder button to on. Little did I know that what I turned on was the Word of God. I wasn't able to put two and two together until later after I got saved. I pushed the tape recorder on Matthew.

And as I was listening to Matthew, all of a sudden the car is driving. And then all of a sudden, the demon left. I am listening to the Word of God.

Now the fear I have leaves. I am freely able to drive home.

When I pulled up into my driveway, I am exhausted. I quickly get into bed and am lying on my back trying to get to sleep. I'm trying to relax, while still thinking about the many kinds of things which have been part of my day.

Because my business involves sales, I've been at all kinds of seminars about using mind over matter to keep good focus. They taught me about being positive in thinking and all that stuff.

Then suddenly, I'm seeing in the spirit realm again and I'm thinking, "Oh, my God, what is going on?"

Lying on my bed, I look up and there's this same demon figure with his eyes glaring at me. He's right there on the wall. Right there in my room.

It says to me, "You're going to die." I am freezing with fear. Quickly I decided to apply my mind over matter tactic against this demon. So I told it, "I'm not going to die."

I learned through these seminars if you "say it and believe it, you'll receive it." As I repeat "I'm not going to die. I'm not going to die…" the demon's piercing eyes are staring at me and I'm shaking with fear. And it says, "You're going to die."

STOP AND HEAR ME VERY CAREFULLY:

You're going to learn something really powerful about the supernatural. It's about saying things like: I feel cold coming on. Well, I hope I don't get the flu. I won't even apply for that grant or scholarship. I'll never get it. I'll never have the money to go on that mission trip.

If the devil can get you to start saying what he says he's got you.

What you say with your mouth is so important. When you line up your mouth and your tongue, and your beliefs with what Satan says, he's got you. He is always a liar and a deceiver.

The demon tells me over and over, "You're going to die." While I'm trying to fight him with my mind over matter, "No, I'm not. No, I'm not."

Amazingly, within a few seconds, he has somehow compelled me to say with my own lips, "I'm going to die." He is saying, "You're going to die." I am now whispering, "I am going to die."

Next see how the demon changes what he says. It's no longer "You are going to die." It's "You are dying."

I'm trying to fight it. I'm staring into these piercing eyes, dark form, ugly, cold creepy thing. I'm repeating, "I'm going to die." But within minutes now I am saying, "I am dying."

Then the words are changed again. The demon said, "You are dead."

ARE YOU LISTENING TO ME?

You must become watchful. If you give the devil an inch, he will take a mile. Keep on giving little bits and soon he'll take it all. Satan comes only to kill, steal and destroy. He wants to take all of us out.

The devil's primary mission is to lead you and me straight on down to the pit of hell.

God desires you and me to freely live in the realm of the supernatural. Jesus said He came that we may have life, and have life more abundantly.

Within a few minutes I have no strength. I have not been saved, remember? They cast the devils out of me. But I had not yet received Jesus into my heart. I have no power over this demonic spirit. And pretty soon it says, "You are dying." Again I fought it for a while. Pretty soon I'm staring at it.

Pretty soon I am in an unexplainable trance. It has control over me. It's saying, "You are dead." It's saying, "You are dead, you are dead." And within a few minutes I'm becoming very complacent. I have lost the will to live. I don't care anymore. Now I am saying, "I am dead, I am dead; I am dead."

Then I said to myself, "In the morning my three children are going to come into this bedroom and they're going to find their mother dead." I just repeated those words aloud over and over.

The demon left where he was and came straight to me.

Immediately he got on top of me and started choking me so much I couldn't breathe.

I knew I was dying. Soon I realized I was about to take my last breath.

But I thank God I started to realize something, because I could have been dead that very moment. My children would have had a mother who was dead.

As I am gasping before taking my one last breath, I feel something coming up from deep inside of me. I don't understand all the things of the supernatural. But I know I am experiencing having this little voice come rising up from down deep inside.

I am gasping, "It was Jesus." That's it. Just the Name of Jesus. It was Jesus. Barely could I get that Jesus out.

And then I said Jesus a little bit louder. And when I said Jesus the second time this thing on my throat had to let go.

Then I yelled, "Jesus!" When I yelled Jesus the third time, my room became brighter than the sun. I can't explain it.

I've never seen anything so bright in my life. It was like a bright, white light. It was huge. The whole room lit up. But it wasn't gold. It was white, a beautiful white. Then all of a sudden, this fear totally left.

The last thing I remember is my whole body was covered with sweat beads. The heat in that room was so intense. I was truly experiencing God's Glory. I don't recall anything else until morning.

❦ The Day I Really Received Jesus ❦

When morning came, I woke up. I usually am up at seven to get my children off to school, but when I looked at the clock in my room it was almost 8:30 AM. I said, "Oh, my God. My kids have left!" Then I got up and went in the other room. They had made an awful mess, with cereal all over the place. They'd already gotten their lunch made and went to school.

I remember sitting down in my kitchen and having a cup of coffee. I have no remembrance of yesterday's events yet. Suddenly I am having an Open Vision.

In the vision was a huge video screen as big as my house. The Lord was showing me a quick video overview of my whole life. He had me seeing everyone who had ever witnessed to me from when I was a child, all the way up to when my neighbor Betty witnessed to me and shared the Scriptures with me.

I remember her getting to the Scriptures: "Jesus loves you." "He died for you." Then every scripture Betty ever taught me, along with the scriptures in the video, came flying towards me – and then came inside me.

Up to then I don't even remember the devil tried to kill me last night.

But now, all of a sudden, I was yelling, "O My God. I went to that Full Gospel Meeting yesterday, and they cast the devil out of me. And last night the devil tried to kill me!"

I remembered that when I called out the Name of Jesus, it was in *The Name of Jesus* which made the devil leave.

Immediately I came to a point where I was calling on the Name of Jesus!

The second time the Name just leapt out from my throat. The third time I let out the name of Jesus, I realized Jesus had set me free! I jumped up and ran into my bedroom. Then I dropped on my knees like I was flying into home plate.

Then I was saying out loud: "**O My God! You've been there all of my life, God.**

"You were there all my life! You were there when I was a little girl. You were there protecting me when I was being sexually abused. You were there when I was in great trouble.

"You were there when I was thrown out on the street with my three babies.

"You were there all the time!"

Then kneeling right where I was by my bed. I said, "Dear Jesus, Come into my heart. Be my Lord; be my Saviour. I'll live for You; I'll die for You; I'll love You always; I'll serve You.

"I will let You take charge of my life...."

Since that moment in time, I have never been the same; because I was translated out of the Kingdom of Satan into the kingdom of God!

❥ Ministers Came For Dinner ❦

When I lived in Kennewick, Washington I was privileged to be able to host a spaghetti dinner for several people who were in town for a Minister's Conference for people who had been ordained under John G. Lake's Ministry. Wilford Reidt and his wife Gertrude, the son-in-law and daughter of the great John G. Lake, presided over the Ministerial Fellowship. It was a special time, because most of the guests were from all over the United States and other countries.

While I was in the kitchen cooking the spaghetti, all the pastors were in the other room praying for the United States and other nations. Then suddenly when I quietly entered the room where they were, some unidentified force hit me as hard as can be right in the middle of my chest. It hit me with such force I fell straight forward on the floor.

All of the wind was blown out of me; I was unable to speak. Meanwhile most of those there in the room were lying on the floor not far away, doing deep intercessory prayer.

Because I could only talk in my mind, I was saying, "God, please let someone here know a Demon attacked me and I can't breathe."

Within a few minutes, one of the pastors came over and was saying, "Satan, get off of Joan right now. Get off right now in the Name of Jesus!" I immediately came up for air.

I was free. Jesus set me free; although the demon left a black and blue mark on my chest. Over the years I have had many experiences with demons and casting out demons.

God desires you to walk in the supernatural with all the power and authority God has given you so that you too can go and pray for the sick and cast out demons.

❥ Demons in the Philippines ❦

One time when I did Ministry in the Philippines, I was given the pleasure of preaching at the church in Manila, which was given to Lester Summerall, where David Summerall was then the pastor.

Years before, a desperate family had asked Lester Summerall to come pray for their little girl. For over a year their child had been plagued daily by demons which were biting her to the extent of leaving teeth marks. You could see the teeth marks on her body.

Despite exhaustive efforts made from many sources, nothing worked. Nobody they consulted had been able to totally set her free!

Finally Lester Summerall prayed for her and cast out several demons and the little girl was set free.

Because the child's family was somewhat well known, the media learned of it. The deliverance session was very widely covered in the press, on radio and even on TV.

The people were so blessed that they wanted Lester Summerall to set up his ministry in Manila. They wound up giving him a building there which covered a whole city block. It became the church where David Summerall then pastored, and where I was preaching.

STOP AND THINK:

That little girl was getting bitten by demons. Bite marks were on her body! Demons are real!

❥ Car Wreck Miracle ❦

I was only 17 years old and at a High School dance. A guy I had a crush on asked to dance with me. He danced with me a few times and then he said, "I will take you for a ride in my new car!"

He took me out into the boondocks and wanted "Something." I told him I was not that sort of girl. So he got mad and said, Well, I will just take you back to the dance then."

We were in the car and he pushed the gas pedal down. I am terrified of speed. So when I saw the speedometer go up to 70 and then 80, then 90 and hit One Hundred Miles an Hour, I am just desperately hanging on to the door. All of a sudden I looked forward – the road was washed away.

The next thing I knew I was in a hospital with a broken back, cracked head and broken pelvis. I hear someone telling me I will never be able to have children. I may never walk. I was in that hospital for over three months.

Years flew by. I was now 29. Unbelievably I was in another car wreck! My follow-up treatment included visits to a chiropractor.

The Chiropractor told me, "Your back is already so disintegrated!" He shows me all the x-rays. My back is so bad I might have to be in a wheelchair. As if that weren't enough, I am wearing a body brace. Plus I had a neck brace too, because I have whiplash in my neck.

Then the chiropractor said, "You are getting worse." I can hardly walk or do anything.

About that time, Betty, my neighbor who led me to the Lord came to the house. She said, "You need to go with me to a healing meeting." She is so persistent that she gets me to go with her.

When we come into the meeting you don't need three dreams and a vision to see something is wrong with me. The evidence is clear; I am wearing both a body brace and a neck brace.

The man who was in charge of the Bible study comes over and says, "Would you like me to pray for you?" My inside voice was saying, "No. Not Really." Nevertheless, I sort of caved in and said, "Yes."

The leader of the Bible study and the whole group laid hands on me and prayed for me. As they all get through praying, I hear the Leader say, "There."

I looked up at him and I said, "Okay. Are you happy now that you prayed for me?" and he said, "Do I detect sarcasm?" My quick answer was, "Look, I let you pray for me and that's enough! Okay?"

It's now time for me to keep my appointment with the chiropractor who will take x-rays of my body. Earlier he had said my back was deteriorating. I might soon have to face being in a wheelchair.

After he takes one set of x-rays, I wondered why he took the trouble to take a second set.

After I'd waited a bit, he came and said, "Now come on in to my office." As I went to sit down, he looked at me and said, "I don't know what to tell you." He picks up the two sets of x-rays off his desk saying, "Let me show you something".

He puts an x-ray on the screen. "Here are your x-rays taken the day we started treating you." He pointed to sections, as he explained, "Here we see where your back was broken and here is where your fifth lumbar was broken. Over here we can see all these spots where your body has been damaged."

I said, "Yes, I see how it was."

Then he picked up the second set of x-rays taken less than an hour before. He puts these up on the screen. It was clear these pictures were the same parts of my neck and back. He said, "Now let's go over today's new x-rays. According to these, you have never had your back broken. Right now, there is not one broken bone in your body."

He added, "I am a physician with a Doctorate in Chiropractics. There is no way I can explain what we are seeing. It is like a miracle!"

I repeat, "Did you just say Miracle? A week ago Monday, I went to a Healing Meeting. People prayed. Then some of them came over and laid hands on my neck and back and prayed specifically that I would be healed in the Name of Jesus."

My clearly befuddled Chiropractor said, "I can't understand how this has happened to you. All I can tell you is you don't need to come back to me. You are now totally healed!"

Thanks to Jesus!

I was overwhelmed and remembered Betty telling me that if I just had faith I would be healed. Now I suddenly found myself just as amazed as my Chiropractor. I had no faith but God responded to the faith of those who prayed for me and Jesus healed me.

❥ Business Miracle ❦

This next story is about prospering. You can't prosper if you don't give. You cannot have prosperity if you're not a giver. That's all there is to it.

God's will is to prosper you in everything you do. After getting saved and having all the demons come out of me, I was running a business as well as trying to raise my children.

I know what it was like to be poor. I know what it was like to be homeless. I know what it was like to be thrown out on the streets with three babies.

I was thrown out on the street when I was two months pregnant. A total stranger came and took me in so I wouldn't have to live on the street. I was poverty stricken. I know what it's like to starve in order to feed my babies.

Now I had it in my heart to be really rich. I wanted a big fancy house, with a really expensive car plus all of the benefits of being rich.

But after I accepted Jesus, something wonderful happened inside. No longer did I want to be rich to buy things for me. I wanted to prosper so that I could give in to the Kingdom of God and write $10,000 checks for ministries.

My friend Betty, who led me to the Lord started tutoring me. Thank God for her tutoring.

She said, "Joan, you can't just work, work, work to make all this money. You have to start being discipled." So she continued with Bible studies and taking me to meetings.

At one of those prayer meetings, the man in charge told me to be specific when I prayed. So I prayed specifically, "Lord, I want to be rich and have my own company. That way I will have lots of money so that I can give into the Kingdom of God. I want to just give and give into Your Kingdom."

About that time the man of God came and placed his hands on my head and said, "God has heard your heartfelt prayer."

The moment he spoke, I heard God say to me: "Before this week is out you will own your company."

At the time, I was working for a company for eight years and was now in a top managerial position. The next step was to be the owner of my own franchise.

In this company you had to be in the top 10 in the United States to even qualify for a franchise. Right now I was in the top 30 range.

Remember, I got saved at a Full Gospel Businessmen's monthly meeting. From then on I was a regular attendee.

In my job I received two paychecks a month. On the fifteenth I got a commission check, which I now simply endorsed over and put into the Full Gospel offering basket. I had little or no knowledge about what tithing or offerings were about. I simply had a heart to give into God's Kingdom.

From the time of my first offering, the amount on my pay checks started to skyrocket and my business shot right up. Soon I was in the number two position in the United States.

It was at the prayer meeting, where I heard God tell me I would own my own company before the week was over. It was held on a Monday night. Where I worked, the system was that those who received a franchise had to relocate to wherever the franchise opened up.

The night of the Prayer Meeting, I went home and told my children, "We're moving!"

The next day I even called to arrange for a moving van. I told my mom, all my relatives and all those who worked for me, "I'll be moving really soon!"

They said, "Where are you moving?"

I said, "I don't know." Most of them responded by telling me in one way or another they thought I was suddenly crazy!

The next Friday, my company had me fly to Utah. I was asked to be the keynote speaker at their annual meeting because I was number two in the country.

After I checked into the hotel, my boss called and asked me to join in a private conference. My boss said there were some people who wanted to talk with you.

When I got there, I met the World President and the United States President of the company I was working for. Interestingly enough one of these men was Mormon and the other was Jewish.

They unfolded a map and laid it on the table. They told me somebody has retired and there is a franchise opening. They pointed to the map saying, "Fly up there and see if you want to take this franchise." They were pointing to the Tri-Cities of Kennewick, Pasco and Richland in Washington State.

I looked into their eyes, and said, "Is there any chance another opening could come up between now and Monday?"

They said, "No, not at all."

I said, "I don't need to go see the territory. I'll just say, yes."

They said, "Nobody's ever accepted one of our franchises without going to check it out first!"

I said, "Monday at a Prayer Meeting God told me I would have my own franchise before next Monday. So there is no reason for me to go check things out."

Next they opened up the contract and explained to me that I'd have to pay $218,000 for the other people's inventory plus the franchise price of $250,000.

I said to them I don't have any money.

They said, "Okay."

They left and went into another room. They were gone about ten minutes. When they came back they both said, "We have no idea why we are doing this. We have never done this before.

"We are going to let you take over the franchise now. We are going to give you an interest free loan, with seven years to pay it off.

"You and your family can go up there and move in as soon as you get packed."

God is so wonderful. My children and I moved to Washington State. I took over the business which was a million dollar business.

The first month we were there, Mount St. Helens erupted and the whole mountain blew over where our territory was located. We were buried in ashes. Cars wouldn't run, it was total chaos.

While that Mountain was erupting all over us, there was a world-wide competition in my company to see who could sell the most products that month.

Despite all the chaos including being buried in the ash, we won the Competition!

Because we won, I was invited to be the keynote speaker at their next Convention. They asked me to share the secret of my success.

I stood in front of about six thousand people and said, "The secret of my success is this: 'Seek ye first the Kingdom of God and His righteousness and all these things will be added unto you.'"

All the people were looking at me thinking what does this have to do with our Company?

I shared with everyone that I used Biblical principles about how to treat my employees. That is why my business was continually so successful.

Over the years which followed, I remember praying to God, "Lord, any time you want me to give up the fancy house and all these luxury things, I will gladly give them up to be in full-time ministry."

Then years later, in the middle of the night, while I was preaching in Virginia Beach, the Lord woke me up and said, "It is time for you to give up your business. I am putting you into full-time ministry."

I said to God, "I make a lot of money. I don't want to give this up for just a year or two." So I said, "Lord will I be preaching when I'm 35." He said, "Yes." "Will I be preaching when I'm ... 40, 50, 55."

He said, "You'll be preaching until the day I take you."

I said, "That settles it." God put me into full-time ministry.

When I said my farewell speech to all those who worked for me in my business, plus the new couple who were taking over the business, I shared the whole plan of salvation with them and gave them my little yellow book which also gave them the plan of salvation.

So God took me from rags and being homeless on the street, to being rich and having a fancy house to being a full-time minister. God knows how to prosper us in this world supernaturally.

When I left the business, God told me to invest all my money into His Kingdom, which I did.

CHAPTER 3
Healing and Deliverance Miracles

We are teaching *When the Supernatural Becomes Natural* because God wants us to walk in the realm of the Supernatural. Healings are supernatural. Deliverance is supernatural. In this chapter we are going to be learning that healings and deliverance are for today.

There are so many people who don't believe healings are for today. So if any of you have questions about whether the Lord wants to heal people today, let's read.

Matthew 8:1-3

When He had come down from the mountain, great multitudes followed Him. And behold, a leper came and worshiped Him, saying, "Lord, if You are willing, You can make me clean." Then Jesus put out His hand and touched him, saying, "I am willing; be cleansed." Immediately his leprosy was cleansed.

Jesus is saying, I want to heal you. God wants us to be healed and have great faith. Let's read.

Matthew 8:5-10,13

Now when Jesus had entered Capernaum, a centurion came to Him, pleading with Him, saying, "Lord, my servant is lying at home paralyzed, dreadfully tormented."

And Jesus said to him, "I will come and heal him."

The centurion answered and said, "Lord, I am not worthy that You should come under my roof. But only speak a word, and my servant will be healed. For I also am a man under authority, having soldiers under me. And I say to this one, 'Go,' and he goes; and to another, 'Come,' and he comes; and to my servant, 'Do this,' and he does it."

When Jesus heard it, He marveled, and said to those who followed, "Assuredly, I say to you, I have not found such great faith, not even in Israel!

... Then Jesus said to the centurion, "Go your way; and as you have believed, so let it be done for you." And his servant was healed that same hour.

So what is God saying? He wants us to have great faith and He wants us to walk in the miraculous and see healings.

❥ Pendleton Prison ❦

Now I'm going to share a little story about my husband Marty and his cousin who was in jail. His other cousin, Terry, was the sister of the one who is in jail.

Marty and I were preaching in the Pendleton, Oregon area having a tent revival. The pastor of the church in Pendleton said he goes into the prison all the time in Pendleton. Marty found out his cousin was there in that prison. He said, "See if the pastor can take you in on his day and you can try to get my cousin saved and be filled with the Holy Ghost."

All the inmates came into the Chapel Service. I did not know which one was Marty's cousin, but Marty said his cousin would nod to me. I just preached my heart out about Jesus. I didn't ask them to come forward. I had them just raise their hands where they were sitting. Thirty to forty people accepted Jesus. There might have been about a hundred men in this meeting.

Then I started teaching on the Baptism of the Holy Ghost. I didn't know all the rules for the prison. I said, "How many of you want to be filled with the Holy Spirit?" Well, there were about 30 men who raised their hands. Now, so you can understand it, behind me there's a big window one story up. There are guards up there in a little room so they could see this room and all the different rooms. They could look from room to room to see what's happening. There were two guards up there, one man guard and a woman guard.

I asked the inmates how many wanted to receive the Baptism of the Holy Spirit. About 30 of them came up to the front. They surrounded me and I started leading them in a prayer for the Baptism of the Holy Spirit. They started falling out under the Power of

God. It just started happening supernaturally and nobody touched them. As they started speaking in tongues they began falling all over the place except for a few of them.

When the guard turned back to see what was going on, he saw me surrounded by men while other men were on the floor. He thought, "What was going on?" He was about to hit the alarm to shut down the whole prison. But the woman guard had been watching the whole thing and she said, "No, no. Don't hit the alarm. They're not attacking her. She looks like she's attacking them."

But I wasn't attacking them. They were all being filled with the Holy Spirit. God's anointing was touching them!

❧ Miracle at AGLOW ❧

I came back home to Marty and I told him not only his cousin, but a whole bunch of men were saved and filled with the Holy Spirit. He said, while I was gone he had been on the phone with another cousin Terry, the sister of the man in prison who had just received Jesus.

My husband has great faith. He is so wonderful. I just love him.

Marty said, "While you were there I've been on the phone with my cousin, Terry. She is the president of the *AGLOW* chapter and she's so discouraged, she's about to close the chapter and just give up. I told her,

No, don't give up. I tell you what, I'm going to send you a gift."

I said, "What gift?" Marty said, "I told her the gift was you and that I would send you there tomorrow."

The next day at the meeting I saw they had people there from the local hospital. They'd gotten people who had checked themselves out of the hospital to come to this meeting. The place was packed. It was a little room but it was filled with people.

So I preached my heart out about healing, deliverance and Jesus. People received Jesus and were filled with the Holy Ghost. I had a prayer line for people to be healed. A lot of people fell under the power of God; some didn't but God did what He wanted to do. Remember we're only vessels for God to use.

Later as the meeting was ending, a young lady came up to me and she had this big boot on her foot. She said, "My foot's hot. My foot's on fire!" I said, "Don't worry about it. It's just the Lord healing you."

About an hour later the same lady comes to our book table and said, "My foot is still burning. My foot is just burning and burning." I said, "Don't worry about it. It just means that God is healing you."

When I returned home three hours later, Marty said, "Some lady called who said you have to talk to her. It's really important."

It was the lady whose foot was on fire. When I talked to her she said, "When I came home several hours after the service where you prayed for me, my foot was still on fire. It was so on fire that if I would have put my foot in a bucket of cold water the water would have gone sizzle, sizzle, sizzle from the heat that was in my foot."

Just before coming to AGLOW, she had foot surgery and they had to cut off part of her foot, the side part of her foot not the whole bottom part. She had a special boot to keep her from tipping over.

When she got home, the Lord had grown out her foot. Where it had been cut off it was all restored, brand new. She never had to wear that boot brace again because the Lord just created a brand new part of that foot where it had been cut.

I believed with all my heart that much of what went on at AGLOW was because Marty had pumped faith into his cousin Terry. She in turn told people about the Miracle Service so that people came to the meeting with high expectations.

When you have high expectations of what God is going to do and you have great faith, and you go to pray for people, you need to first build their faith by sharing Jesus and testimonies. Build their faith and then their faith will be strong and they can receive their miracle.

My husband Marty has great faith and had helped build up those people's faith for a miracle.

Romans 10:17

So then faith comes by hearing, and hearing by the word of God.

It was like the story of the centurion who said Jesus did not have to come to his house. Jesus just had to speak the word and his servant would he healed. Jesus marveled at the great faith he had. God's word says to us.

Hebrews 11:1

Now faith is the substance of things hoped for, the evidence of things not seen.

Hebrews 11:6

But without faith it is impossible to please Him, for he who comes to God must believe that He is, and that He is a rewarder of those who diligently seek Him.

Well, that's very important. So, we need to know that we have that kind of faith. God desires to use you and all of us!

❧ Raising the Dead ❧

My son Alan was raised from the dead. Now I never thought God would ever use me to raise somebody from the dead. But so far, God used me to see two people raised from the dead. But I'm not going to share the other story now. I'm just going to share about my son Alan.

When my son was about eighteen years old, he wanted to do his own thing. So he got his own apartment where he lived with a couple of guys who were his friends.

In the middle of the night I received a phone call. It was about three in the morning from one of the teenagers my son was living with. He said, "Alan's dead, Alan's dead, Alan's dead."

I said, "What? He's dead?"

I said, "I'll be right there."

You don't know when there's going to be a disaster. You don't know when God's going to have you pray for somebody in an accident on the side of the road. You don't know when God needs to use you so you need to be prepared 24/7. That means we need to have times of worship and time to get into the word of God because you don't know until you're in a situation like this, what is in you.

As soon as I get in the car I said, "Oh God, he's my son." It was amazing. I got in the car and all of a sudden I started prophesying while I'm driving. I'm driving and proclaiming, "Alan shall live. He shall live and not die. He shall live and not die."

I'm prophesying, "Live Alan, live." I'm calling, "Live Alan. You shall live and not die."

I'm saying that and I'm also saying, "Not because my son deserves to live, not because he is serving You but because of Your mercy and because of Your grace. Oh God, spare my son. Let Him live so he can call on the name of the Lord and be saved."

Great faith is in me. Scriptures are just coming out of me – faith scriptures and more faith scriptures. The whole twenty minutes while I'm driving there God was building my faith. When I get there two policemen had already arrived because the teenagers had called the police. The policemen were trying to find the apartment.

I saw them. It was still dark and I said, "Follow me." So they followed me and we went upstairs to Alan's apartment. We all walked in together, the two policemen and me. We walked in and there's my son laying on the floor. Just laying on the floor. The two teenage boys were both talking to me at the same time trying to tell me why he's dead.

They're trying to explain all this and the policemen were talking at the same time. My son was laid out on the floor and the two policemen were doing whatever they were doing and I just looked up at all four of them and said, "Shut up! I have to hear God."

I walked out of the apartment and stood in the hallway. I said, "God, I need to hear you. I need to hear you right now, God. What do I do?" And I heard God speak. I'm telling you, there's nothing more wonderful than when the word of God confirms it and then faith kicks in. Not just a normal faith. The supernatural faith kicked in. I heard God actually speak to me audibly. You'll always remember what He said.

This is the word, "Go in. Put your hands in the middle of his back. Pray for him. He'll be up walking by noon." These were the exact words. No extras.

"Go in and put your hands in the middle of his back. Pray for him. He'll be up walking by noon."

I walked back in and told the policemen, "Alan needs to be rolled over." The policemen said, "We're not allowed to touch him before the paramedics come with all their stuff."

The teenage boys said, "Oh, we're not going to touch him either."

I saw they weren't going to do anything. So I turned to the two teenagers who were his roommates and I said with boldness and authority, "I'm his mother. Roll his body over now!" And they looked at the policemen. I said, "Now!"

They rolled Alan over and he was stiff. I don't know how to explain this but his body was as stiff as a board. They rolled him over so he is face down because the Lord told me to put my hands in the middle of his back. I looked at the two policemen and the two teenagers and said, "I don't know if you believe in God or not but I do. So you can either pray with me or you can laugh at me but I don't care." I knelt down on my knees over my son's body and I started speaking in tongues. Really loud.

When I put my hands on his back while praying in tongues his whole body jumped off the floor, two or three inches. Just like that. Then I put my hands on him again and I prayed in tongues and it happened again. I did it three times. It's like when they have the paddles they put on people and the whole body jumps. I did it three times.

Then I heard the Holy Spirit say, "Roll him over."

I said to the two teenagers, "Roll him over." They rolled my son over. I got up off my knees, walked over and looked down at my son. All of a sudden his eyes opened. They didn't open normally. They looked like he was gone and now he's back. I looked down at him with his eyes open and I said, "Call me at noon."

I don't know if he remembers, but his roommates told him, "You're supposed to call your mom at noon." I said, "I'm going home."

The policemen replied, "What? You're what?"

I said, "I'm going home."

"Well, aren't you going to wait for the paramedics?" "No."

One of the teenage boys said, "You're doing what?" I said, "I'm leaving."

I left my son on the floor face up and walked out the door and went home.

The phone rang right at twelve. I didn't even say "Hello, who is it?" I just said, "Hi, Alan, how are you?"

He said, "Mom, they told me to call you at noon. They told me what happened." I said to my son, "Alan, the devil's trying to kill you.

"Satan has come to steal and kill. He's been trying to kill you. Remember how you were in a wreck two weeks ago and the Holy Spirit protected you?"

When that accident happened, the Lord showed me a picture of him in a coffin so I started praying and praying. I didn't know why. Then when I got home I found out Alan was on the front page because he and another teenage friend had rolled their car off a cliff and Alan came out of it alive.

Now two weeks later after Alan was raised from the dead I'm having a Bible study in my home. While I'm in the middle of the Bible study, my son came in and said, "I'm sorry, everybody. I have to talk to my Mom now!"

And I'm thinking, "Boy, this had better be good for you to stop the whole Bible study in the middle." He walks up in front of me and now he has everybody's attention, including mine and I'm upset.

He says, "Mom."

I said, "What, Alan?"

He said, "I tried to cross the street a few hours ago and I almost was run over. I can't wait until your Bible Study is over. I want to accept Jesus now. Can I do it?"

And he dropped down on his knees and said, "Mom, what am I supposed to say?" He repeated the sinner's prayer and accepted Jesus Christ into his heart in the middle of the Bible study. I was so happy. We never did finish the Bible study. We just glorified God.

❥ Healing From Lupus ❦

When you walk in the Supernatural, wonderful things happen. Miracles will happen. There are so many kinds of miracles. Let me share several more miracles.

There was a lady who had terrible Lupus disease and was crippled and could hardly walk. She got worse and worse. Her husband loved to go walking. I was preaching a message on love not on healing.

While I preached the message on love, she understood that God loved her and was totally healed.

Now that God healed her and she could walk she said, I'm going to be in a 4 kilometer race with my husband.

So she put a number on her back because you can either walk the race or you can run the race. Her husband was going to run but she was going to walk. She had her number on for the section for the women to walk. Then all of a sudden she changed her mind.

The Lord healed her so she said, "I don't want to walk it, I want to run it."

So they gave her a different number and put her in the women's section to run it. She not only ran the race she won the race, never to go back and be crippled again. It was all because of Jesus.

❥ Healing of Eyes ❦

When I had just started in ministry I was doing a Bible study in my home I also was running a corporation. At one time I had forty managers working for me. I ran a competition among them in which the two top managers will win a shopping spree with me. They each would win 500 dollars worth of clothes.

Darlene, one of the winners of the trip lived about three hours from my house so she spent the night with me. I thought, "We can't leave to go shopping to Portland until I do my Bible study." She's up in the guest room and the Holy Spirit says to me, invite her to your Bible study. Now Darlene is a Catholic woman.

The Holy Spirit said to me, "Darlene has a rare eye disease." I didn't know she had a rare eye disease but the Holy Spirit knew. I said, "She does?" The Lord said, "Yes, so I want you to have her come down to your Bible study and when you spit in her eye she'll be healed."

"When I what? When I spit in her eye she'll be healed." Did I hear this right?

Now, it takes a little bit of guts to know that your top manager is going to tell everybody who works for you that you just spit in her eyes. I didn't even know if she was saved. I know she's a good Catholic. Anyway, I invited her to come down and changed my whole message to about how Jesus made spit and clay and about healing of eyes.

So my whole message is on faith and I want to make sure she's saved so I did an altar call right in the middle of my Bible study.

Darlene did ask Jesus in her heart. Now, I'm trying to get courage and I read all these scriptures on Jesus healing people. I prayed, "Oh Lord Jesus. The people in my Bible study are going to think I'm crazy, too. They'll stop coming."

I just want to let you know that Darlene had great faith.

I said, "Darlene, this morning the Lord told me before the Bible study started that you have a rare eye disease. Is that true?"

She said, "Yes, I do. I've been to specialists and they can't find a cure. It's in the retina." Anyway, she explained it all and then she said, "I'm in terrible pain and they don't know how to fix it." I said, "The Lord said, if I spit in your eyes you'll be healed." She said, "Oh, go ahead." I said, "Really?"

Now, I'm a lady and I want to be lady like. So, I said, "Lord, how do I do this?" The Lord told me to put spit on my two fingers and then put one finger on one eye and the other finger on the other eye and then pray for divine healing for her.

She was instantly healed. To God be the glory. I saw her years later at a fair. She was healed and never had eye problems again.

It took a little faith because you don't know what God might ask you to do. You know, there are mighty men and women of God who have slugged people and thrown people up in the air. You better know you're hearing God because He wants to use us in the miraculous even when it seems to make no sense to you.

❧ "Lady, Come Out of That Wheelchair" ❧

We've had many people healed in the crusades and Marty was a big part of one of them. My husband has great faith. We were doing a tent meeting in Riverside, California and I thought the crusade was over.

The tent meeting lasted a solid week and one lady had come every night. She would roll up front in her wheelchair and I'd pray for people and then she'd roll back to her seat. Every night she'd came up for prayer and every night she still was in the wheelchair.

It was Thursday night and she came up front for prayer. I had prayed for a whole line of people who fell under the power of God and their bodies were all lying down on the floor. People are being healed and crying and weeping. So she's stuck up front. She can't roll back because these people are all over blocking the floor.

But my husband got a word of knowledge from the Holy Spirit and he came up and said to me, "Honey, do you see the lady in the wheelchair?" I said, "Yeah." "You see, tonight she has faith to be healed. Look, she's looking at everybody with joy. She doesn't have her eyes on her own situation. She has faith right now to be healed. Pray for her. Pray for her again, right now." I said, "Okay."

So Marty and I walked over to her. Marty had such great faith that he took off the leg rails so she could stand up and come straight out of that wheelchair. He had faith in advance that she's going to walk and come out of that wheelchair. So he removed these obstacles so she could just jump out of her wheelchair and walk.

I went over and started praying for her. I don't believe in pulling people out of a wheelchair so I had her put her hands on my hands and I started praying. I was just quietly praying. Not even that loud. I just started praying and I knew that I knew that my prayers were going into the Holy of Holies. I prayed: Jesus, Heal her. Jesus, Heal her. I wasn't even saying that out loud.

All of a sudden, she jumped out of that wheelchair. Nobody pulling her out. She jumped out of that wheelchair. She didn't walk, she started dancing! Remember there were people all over the floor. She danced and she would go up in the air and she'd spin. There's no way this lady could've danced this way in the natural. She's dancing. She's mid-air swinging like a ballerina. Not once did she come down and land on anybody's body.

Sometimes her legs came down between people's legs or under their arms but she never once touched anyone. She went from one end of the tent to the other end of the tent and back again dancing and spinning and never stepping on anybody.

She went back to the University of Berkeley, a renowned hospital in California where she'd been getting treatment. We didn't know why she was in the wheelchair but she had Hepatitis C and her liver was at the last stages. She couldn't walk because her muscles were so weak. They had her on a list for a liver transplant. If she didn't get it she would die.

When they tested her, they said to her, "We do not know what has happened to you. Somebody has put a brand new liver into your body and you can be taken off the liver list." Now she's doing wonderfully.

This is years later and she's very active in her church. She has no problems with her liver or kidneys. She was totally miraculously healed. God gave her a brand new liver. My husband had heard; now she has faith. He said, "I perceive she has faith right now for a miracle." She sure did!

❥ Healing From Leukemia ❦

Another miracle is about a little eight year old girl who came to our tent meetings in Port Orchard, Washington. When she came in she was bald. I thought she was a boy. But my husband had great faith and every time I did a prayer line, the little girl was in the line and I'd pray for her. She'd go down under the power of God. Marty didn't want her to get stepped on so he would never let her go back to her seat.

He would just drape her little body and put her on the front seat. When I did another prayer line he would grab her little body and put her on the next prayer line. Marty believes, and I believe, that the more a person is prayed for and stays under the anointing the better it is.

She must have been prayed for six or seven times. At the end of the service I had an altar call for salvation. About twenty-five people came up for salvation. The little girl was one of them.

There was a lady standing with a baby in her arms and Marty was standing right beside me. All of a sudden my spirit sensed a twister coming from the far end corner of the tent. We had big banners, but the banners weren't moving yet I could sense this twister coming.

I could sense in my spirit that it was getting closer and closer and I'm doing a prayer for salvation. Dear Lord, come into my heart be my Lord and Savior. I never even got the whole prayer finished when all of a sudden there was this urgency in my heart to take the baby out of the lady's arms. So I grabbed the baby from the lady and handed the baby to Marty. About that time, the twister hit them all and it spun these people in circles. It's like a little whirlwind. It spun the people and they went all over the floor like a big circle just laid out.

I hadn't finished leading them to the Baptism of the Holy Spirit yet. I got as far as, "Dear Jesus, come into my heart." Some of them had fallen, and by the time they hit the floor many of them were speaking in tongues. Some of them were crying; some of them were shaking; some of them were weeping violently. It was late and we ended the tent meeting but people were still on the floor. Some people were there for a long time but little by little they started to get up and leave.

The last one to get up was the little girl. She must have been on the floor for about forty-five minutes. She was on her back, just shaking and trembling with tears running down the side of her face.

I finally went and sat down on the tent floor beside her. After about 45 minutes, she opened her eyes and looked at me and said "Where did he go?" I said, "Where did who go?"

She said again, "Where did he go?" I said, "Who, honey?"

She said, "Jesus. Jesus was with me and Jesus came to me and he told me don't worry little girl. You won't die. I've healed you."

We didn't know what she had, but we knew she had no hair. She had Leukemia and the doctors told her family there's nothing they can do. She's had so many blood transfusions that she can't have anymore. Enjoy her for the next few weeks. Her parents said they were willing to try anything.

They heard that miracles were happening at this tent meeting, so they came. The whole family accepted Jesus. When the little girl went back to the doctor for tests, there was no trace whatsoever of Leukemia in her body. She was totally healed.

Take time to read

Isaiah 53:1-5

Who has believed our report? And to whom has the arm of the Lord been revealed?
For He shall grow up before Him as a tender plant, And as a root out of dry ground.
He has no form or comeliness; And when we see Him, There is no beauty that we should desire Him.
He is despised and rejected by men, A Man of sorrows and acquainted with grief. And we hid, as it were, our faces from Him; He was despised, and we did not esteem Him.

Surely He has borne our griefs And carried our sorrows; Yet we esteemed Him stricken, Smitten by God, and afflicted.
But He was wounded for our transgressions, He was bruised for our iniquities; The chastisement for our peace was upon Him, And by His stripes we are healed.

Look especially at the last verse where he was wounded for our transgressions. He was bruised for our iniquity. He was chastised so we could achieve our peace. And by his stripes and by his beating on his back, we were healed.

You know they beat him with the cat o'nine tails. I was told that at the end of the whip there were little bones which cut the skin.

Doctors say that all major diseases come from thirty-nine main causes. Each has a family of smaller diseases. Isn't that amazing. Every one of those stripes and each of the little ones were paid for by the stripes on the back of Jesus. We were healed. All we have to do is have faith to receive it because our healing was already done two thousand years ago on the cross.

❧ Miracle of Deliverance ☙

This is a story about a lady named Jackie who was a Satanist. She attended a Satanic church and she worshiped Satan.

Now it's very strange that a Satan worshiper would come to a Christian church. But this lady came to the church where I was preaching and sat in the third row. As the anointing got stronger and I started praying for people, she got up several times to try to leave. But the ushers would not let her leave.

When the service was over she handed me a note but I didn't have time to read it. I opened it when I got back to the Pastor's house.

It read:

"I came to church today because I love my cat and I don't want to kill my cat. Nobody in the world loves me. My family is all gone. I have only one thing in the world that I love. It is my cat. I've had my cat for a long time.

"I am a Satan worshiper and the Satanic church wants to test me to make sure I'll be faithful to an alliance with Satan. So they told me that I have to kill my cat and I have to bring my dead cat back in and show them that I killed my cat.

"I don't want to kill my cat. But I'm afraid if I don't obey them and don't kill my cat they'll hurt me. So I thought maybe if I came to church we could find some way that I don't have to kill my cat."

Her love for her cat is what brought her to church. So, I showed the letter to the pastor. We started fasting and praying for her.

It was the last night of the revival and I prayed, "Oh, God, You've got to reach her somehow tonight."

At the end of the service I felt the anointing was really strong. I said, "Jackie, God loves you and I love you." She starts shaking her head as if to say, "No." I said, "God doesn't want you to kill your cat. God loves you much more than you love your cat."

As I walked towards her, she came towards me and I hugged her. When I hugged her she started crying. "I don't want to kill my cat, I love my cat." She was really crying and I said, "Jesus loves you the same way. Will you accept Jesus?"

She was very bold and said to me, "If I come to Jesus, and I want to, and I pray right now and come to Jesus and they find out, they're going to hurt me. I've been in that church long enough for me to know what they do. So, who's going to protect me? I live by myself."

I asked the Pastor to come over and I said, "Will you, if Jackie asks Jesus into her heart, be here for her if she needs to come to your house because she is running for her life?" He said, "Yes."

I went one step further and said, "Do you really mean it?" And he said, "Yes." Jackie said, "Okay. I'm going to do it. I'm going to ask Jesus into my heart. I don't really want to be in the Satanic Church. They scare me. I've seen the things they do."

That night Jackie renounced Satan, was set free of some demons and received Jesus. She moved in with the Pastor and his wife for a while.

I saw her 10 years later and she was still serving God.

God wants you to step out believing in the finished work of the cross. Let God use you to see miracles.

❥ Healing in India ❧

1 Corinthians 1:17,18

For Christ did not send me to baptize, but to preach the gospel, not with wisdom of words, lest the cross of Christ should be made of no effect.
For the message of the cross is foolishness to those who are perishing, but to us who are saved it is the power of God.

God wants us to live by faith and walk in His power.

The Bible says.

Romans 1:16

For I am not ashamed of the gospel of Christ, for it is the power of God to salvation for everyone who believes, for the Jew first and also for the Greek.

God wants us to walk in divine healing.

I was on another mission trip, this time to India to do tent meetings. We were praying for 5,000 people every night. There were four of us on the team and we prayed for people every night. Great and wonderful miracles were happening. There was a lady who was all bent over. She couldn't straighten up. When she came where I was praying I took my fist and hit her on the back and with my other hand, hit her on the forehead.

I hit her hard and after I did I thought, "Oh my God! Why did I do that?" It was like when Smith Wigglesworth once slammed somebody in the stomach and the cancer left.

I hit this bent over woman on the forehead and hit her on the back at the same time. Suddenly she walked away standing up and straight.

I thought to myself, "No wonder the Lord had me hit her, she was a phony. Look how fast she straightened up."

That's what I thought, but the next night she got up and came on the platform in front of 5,000 people to give her testimony and she was pointing at me. I thought, "Oh God she's probably going to tell everybody in the whole congregation that I hit her last night. She slugged me last night."

I thought I was truly getting in trouble with the missionary team.

Instead she said, "That lady prayed for me last night, and Jesus touched me. I've been bent over like this for 27 years unable to stand up straight. Look, I'm straight." She straightened up and was healed.

Luke 13:11-16

And behold, there was a woman who had a spirit of infirmity eighteen years, and was bent over and could in no way raise herself up.

But when Jesus saw her, He called her to Him and said to her, "Woman, you are loosed from your infirmity." And He laid His hands on her, and immediately she was made straight, and glorified God.

But the ruler of the synagogue answered with indignation, because Jesus had healed on the Sabbath; and he said to the crowd, "There are six days on which men ought to work; therefore come and be healed on them, and not on the Sabbath day."

The Lord then answered him and said, "Hypocrite! Does not each one of you on the Sabbath loose his ox or donkey from the stall, and lead it away to water it? So ought not this woman, being a daughter of Abraham, whom Satan has bound – think of it – for eighteen years, be loosed from this bond on the Sabbath?"

We need to know that God wants to use each and every one of us to walk in supernatural miracles.

CHAPTER 4
The Vision on a Mission Trip

I'm going to share with you a heavenly vision. Everybody likes glimpses of heaven because that's where God's glory is.

I'm going to share about how God spanked me.

How many of you know that God chastises those He loves? So, I've gotten spanked. I've been getting a lot of spankings from the Lord. But every one I get from the Lord takes me to a higher level. He has to chastise those of us who are a little more stubborn than others. You all know what I'm talking about.

Some of us are stubborn and have to learn to yield to the Holy Spirit and hear the voice of God so we can walk in the Supernatural.

Every now and then God has to rattle our cage and get us in shape.

I'd been asked to go on a trip to Mexico. We flew into Mexico City. Then we went way up into the mountains on a winding mountain pass to do the crusades. I was with some brothers and sisters in the Lord and John G. Lake's son-in-law was with us. His wife Gertrude stayed at home.

We got up into the mountain area where we were being housed. The missionaries we were staying with said to all of us, "We found some people killed and their bodies were cut up with machetes. They were found in ditches. There are Communist groups all over the area and they're stealing property from everybody. Don't go too far off by yourself because if you do you could get into trouble and get killed, especially if you're a Christian."

One day, I decided to go for a little walk, but I didn't realize that I had walked quite so far. I should have stayed in the compound where I knew we were safe. I was on this walk, when all of a sudden I heard jeeps and tanks and lots of engine sounds.

I looked and I could see there was a whole caravan with SWAT signs. I knew I didn't want them to see me so I jumped into some bushes and went deep into them.

While I was there, the Lord gave me an open vision which was very life changing to me. He showed me with a crown on my head that was glorious and beautiful. It was filled with all kinds of stones, emeralds, sapphires, rubies and gems with colors I've never seen. When you have a heavenly vision, the colors are not like the colors here on earth. The colors are more radiant, more beautiful and they're luminous. That's the only way I can explain it.

It was as if the jewels were alive; they just radiated with light coming out of them.

In the vision there was a mud pond in front of me. I watched as every stone popped out and went into the mud and sunk until the crown was totally empty. Then the crown sank too until it was gone and all I can see was mud. I understood what this meant. My soul winner's crown had gone into the mud.

I started crying and saying, "What is this, God? What is this?" The Lord was spanking me and rebuking me. I was a fairly new Christian when this happened and had only been saved for a short time. The Lord said to me, "Yes, you've been a great soul winner and you have many stones in your crown." By that time I've been to India, had big crusades and preached to 5,000 people. I'd also been to the Philippines where I led many people to the Lord.

He said, "But you have lost your reward. You've lost all of it because of the motive of your heart. You want the pats on the back and you want to receive all the glory and all the recognition. Therefore, because your heart has not been pure before Me, you have lost the reward."

I wept and cried and said, "God forgive me. Change my heart God. Make my heart pure. I do care about the lost."

He said, "I know you care about the lost but there are also other motives. They've got to go."

I wept and cried, "God, please forgive me."

Then the vision started up again. All of a sudden I heard the Lord speak to me and He said, "Will you do it my way, Joan? Will you let me, from this day forward, put the stones in the crown instead of you trying to do it?"

I said, "Yes, Lord."

All of a sudden I saw the Lord's hand going over the mud puddle. He didn't have to reach down to get the crown or clean it. As the crown came up out of the mud and it got into Jesus's hands it was glorious and the gold was radiant and totally clean.

The Lord came over to me. I remember feeling Him, but not seeing Him do it. He put that crown on my head. The presence of God was so strong as He put it on my head and said, "Now, do it my way, Joan."

In the next scene in the vision, I was in heaven in a huge room. It was glorious. There were sounds radiating and everything seemed alive. It was bright and gorgeous. All of a sudden I was standing in front of a doorway with curtains.

I was standing there feeling like a little child, which we all are in God's eyes because we are children of God. I was feeling this really exciting energy of heaven going through me. It was like electric currents that were just flowing all over the place.

Suddenly I heard an angel say, "Walk over to me." He had a big satin or velvet pillow, and on it was a crown. I walked over and he put the crown on my head. It was the same crown I'd seen before that the stones had popped out of, but now it had more stones in it. He said to me, "Are you ready, Joan?"

"Yes." But I didn't know what I was supposed to be ready for.

Suddenly I heard the sound of a horn. A huge angel who was at least eighteen feet tall had one of those long horns and he started playing it. It just vibrated everywhere.

Then the angel that was over by me said, "You can go in now." And a door way opened in front of me. As I started to walk through this doorway, the presence of Jesus was so strong that I remembered dropping on my knees. I remembered taking this crown off my head and I went prostrate on the floor on my belly. As I took this crown off I threw it to the feet of Jesus and said, "You are worthy. Oh, Jesus you are worthy, you are worthy." Then I came out of the vision and I was again in the bushes.

When I checked I could see the trucks had gone and I went back to the compound. I'll never forget that vision. God wants you and me to know that He wants us to walk in the realm of the supernatural so that we will be soul winners and cast our crowns at the feet of Jesus.

❧ Missionary Connection ☙

I am now a minister and I'm going to Bible College because the Lord told me to go. I had already been a minister for several years doing missionary trips in the Philippines and different places. I was on several mailing lists and received many ministry newsletters. I kept a particular one and put it in my desk drawer.

Finally, while I'm still in Bible College, I started to clean out my desk drawer and found the newsletter. I heard, "Don't throw that one away." When I picked it up and I held it, I heard the Holy Spirit say, "You are going to minister with this person."

I said, "This newsletter, I'm going to go to minister with the people in this newsletter?"

Now I'm curious. Who are they? Where are they from? I finally opened the newsletter. I had it for months. It was from a pastor of a leper colony. Then I exclaimed, "Oh, my God. I'm going to preach at the leper colony."

At that time I was getting ready to go to the Philippines with a team of ministers in five months. Gus Pitt, who was the Bible Dean at that time, had just come back from a trip to the Philippines. After school Gus and all the students went to lunch, I joined them and found out all about his trip to the Philippines.

We're sitting down for lunch and Gus said, "I've met this lady in the Philippines, Joan. You have got to meet her. She is like a duplicate of you."

He starts to tell me her name and I said, "Her name is Sister Tinyo."

Gus looks at me and says, "How is it that you know Sister Tinyo?"

I said, "Is that her name?"

He says, "Yes, it is! But how is it that you know Sister Tinyo?"

I said, "I don't know her, all I know is I've been trying to throw away her newsletter, but the Lord told me that I'm going to meet her and minister with her in the leper colony."

Now it's time for me to go to the Philippines. So I asked the person I'm going to the Philippines with, "Can I break away from the rest of the crowd and go minister with Sister Tinyo for a week and go to the leper colony?"

He said, "No you can't. You're part of the team and I have everything scheduled. When you're part of the team you submit to the people in authority. You're going to go with us. We've got crusades. We have no time for you to meet this whoever she is."

We get to the Philippines, a lady walks up to the whole team and says, "Are you Brother so and so and Sister so and so?"

"Yes."

"Well the people that were supposed to pick you up today, their jeep broke down. They are way up in the mountains and so they called me because I live here in Manila. My name is Sister Tinyo and I'm here to take you into the mountains."

I'm going like, "Wow!"

She said, "You are Joan Pearce?"

I said, "Yes, and I know all about you because Gus Pitt was here and he told me there was a duplicate of me here."

I said to the team leader, "Oh, please let me go spend time ministering with her." He said "No, it's not in the schedule." But you see God's schedule is different.

So we get way up in the mountains and we're doing crusades and after we're up there two or three weeks, we received word that it's too dangerous to go further up and do the crusade. It was the last crusade before we went back to Manila to go back to the United States.

So the brother that was in charge said to me, "Well Sister Joan, I guess you got your wish. I'll have somebody take you back to Manila and you can spend a week with Sister Tinyo and then she can put you on the plane to go home."

God is the one that orders our footsteps and God wants us to walk in miraculous miracles. Sister Tinyo is very bold. Actually I think she is much bolder than me. I'm going to share three wonderful stories that happened while we were there which are all about the Supernatural.

❧ The Warden and What Happened in Prison ☙

The first thing she lined up was to go into a prison. I thought, "Wow!" This is awesome! I'm on an adventure with God! Hallelujah! So we go to the prison. Boy, it's not like an American prison! I mean it was bad! Bad dudes, bad situation, bad floors, icy. We have to go in where the warden's office is because he's going to tell us what cells we are going to visit.

While we're sitting there, a man comes in and the warden says, "I'll be with you ladies in a minute, just sit here." So we're quietly praying.

Sister Tinyo tells me, "Don't butt in." The man was a prisoner and they're getting ready to release him. A guard comes in with him.

I'm sitting there. I'm not supposed to say anything, but all of a sudden I heard the Holy Spirit say, "Ask the warden if he wants to see this man back in prison or if he wants never to see him again? And that you can guarantee that he won't be back."

The warden was trying to release this inmate and said, "I don't want to see you back here! Every time you leave you're back in within a few weeks!"

All of a sudden I said, "I'm not supposed to be talking.

"But excuse me Sir, Warden. If you would let me have fifteen minutes with him I can guarantee you that he will never be back."

♣ The Warden and the Prisoner ♣

The Warden looked at me and said, "Really? Well I'm tired of seeing him go and come back."

I said, "If you give me fifteen minutes I can guarantee that he will never be back."

And he said, "You have the floor, fifteen minutes." So I'm together with the Warden, the man being released and the guard and I share the plan of salvation. All three of them accept Jesus as their Lord and Saviour!

I have them join hands and they repent and accept Jesus. I said to the prisoner, "Now when you get out find a good church and don't come back. Because you have a helper; you have Jesus now."

When the guard and prisoner left the Warden said, "Now he's going to work with us.

"Look, I know you are scheduled to go in today and talk in the prison but we've just had a riot and we found that there's been shooting and they've been making knives. I just don't feel good about you two ladies being here right now. So I'm sorry."

I said, "Wait, warden please. I'm here from America. I only have this week. Right after Easter I'm flying back to America. I spent a lot of money and I've worked really hard to get my ticket, so don't discourage me.

"God will protect me. God will protect us both.

"He said, "Let me think about it a few minutes. I don't know why I'm doing this. Okay you ladies can go in there but you know this is probably not the best idea. I sure don't want to have some American die in our prison." And so he gives in.

The guard takes us to a cell that has seventy-five prisoners. He puts me and Sister Tinyo in it and locks us in there with no guards. There is nobody there in the cell except us and the prisoners.

It's dirty and the guys are tattooed and they're making gestures. And so I start to preach. I hadn't been preaching for more than five minutes, when all of a sudden every light in that place goes off. You see sparks going everywhere. I'm standing there but it's so dark that Sister Tinyo said, "Sister Joan, it would be wise if you get out of the middle of the room and come over here."

I said, "Talk to me so that I can hear your voice." Guns are firing and people are fighting each other. I didn't know what was going on, but I could see gunfire everywhere.

I walked backwards trying to hear Sister Tinyo's voice, and she says, "I'm here." So I touched her, and I could feel her. All of a sudden, the lights came back on and we could see how God had supernaturally protected us. The prisoners, rapists and murderers, the people who were in prison, had made a wall around us with their bodies.

You see there was no one else to protect us. So God put it on the hearts of these prisoners to make a wall around our bodies to protect us. There were things going on all over the place and the Holy Ghost was with us.

I said to the men, "You could have all been dead five minutes ago. You could have been shot; everyone of you could've been shot and dead! And you'd be in hell!" And I preached Jesus, and I preached it hard and heavily and seventy-five people accepted Jesus Christ. The whole group accepted Jesus Christ as their Lord and Saviour.

When we got out of the cell and went to the Warden's office he said "Oh my God, I forgot you ladies were in there. Oh my God! Thank God you didn't get shot! You didn't get killed!"

So I said, "All of the men accepted Jesus. We have thirty thousand Bibles so do we have permission to give every one of them a Bible?"

"Yes, give everyone of them a Bible."

Then we said. "We have thirty thousand Bibles not seventy-five Bibles. How many prisoners do you have in the other cells?"

And he said, "Two hundred forty."

We said, "Well, can we come back tomorrow?"

He said, "Are you kidding me!? I'm glad that you're alive."

I said, "Yeah, but you accepted Jesus a little while ago remember? You accepted Jesus earlier so you want other people to have what you have. If they accept Jesus it would be a lot calmer prison. There would be a lot less fighting. We have a lot more Bibles and we have Bibles for every single inmate in this whole jail. How many more guys do you have?" "Two hundred forty." "Why don't you let us come back tomorrow?"

Well it's against my better judgement but we went in the next day and about a hundred prisoners accepted Jesus and we gave them all Bibles. Sister Tinyo said to the warden, "They don't know how to use these Bibles. Would it be alright with you if I come once a week and have a Bible study with the entire prison?"

He said, "Yes."

You see, we can live in the realm of the Supernatural when people don't even know why they're letting you go into the jail or why they'd let you give the prisoners a Bible.

You see, God's Kingdom is higher than the things of this world.

When God wants something done it's just going to get done. That's all there is to it.

After this whole experience of being in the jail, I was so pumped up and excited and Sister Tinyo said, "Now you're ready to go into the leper colony!"

I said, "I'm ready."

❧ In the Leper Colony ☙

I prayed to God when I went into the leper colony, "Please don't let me see their sores. Don't let me see their wounds." So into the leper colony we go to give away the rest of the Bibles. I didn't see their leprosy. I hugged them and loved them with pus running on them. With parts of their face falling off. Parts of their legs falling off. And then we went to the infirmary and there were a couple hundred of lepers on cots. They had lost so many parts of their body that they could no longer walk.

I went into the hospital with my interpreter. Sister Tinyo went another way, so I was in there alone with my interpreter. You know that faith comes by hearing the word of God. I spent two hours there because it takes longer when you say a message first in English and then have it translated into Filipino. I spent an hour on scriptures of faith, Jesus and receiving Jesus. I shared with them that Jesus loves them and used the Scriptures about Jesus and faith.

Then I said, "Now I want everyone to pray this prayer." Remember, they couldn't get up. They're all in these cots. Everyone repeated after me: "Dear Jesus, come into my heart. Be my Lord and Saviour." All of them are praying. I don't know if they all meant it, but all of them, a couple of hundred, prayed to accept Jesus.

Then the Lord says, "Now pray for them because they're sick. Their bodies were all covered with leprosy."

Then I shared healing scriptures.

I closed my eyes but I shouldn't have. I said, "Get ready to receive your healing." I put my hands out over all of them and said, "Our Saviour Jesus, you are the great physician. Jesus heals."

I had everybody pray, "I'm healed. Thank you Jesus for healing me."

I had them repeating, "Jesus, touch me now and heal my body." All of a sudden, the Holy Spirit said, "Open your eyes."

When I opened my eyes, a mist from about 6 inches under their cot to about 6 inches above their bodies was this Glory Cloud. I said, "Wow what is that? What is that God?" And He said, "I'm healing them."

We got a letter saying that 32 of the lepers were healed. We don't know how many were really healed but God knows. Nothing is too hard for God. The healing had nothing to do with me and my interpreter; it was a sovereign move of God.

And there's been different times that we've ministered and seen the Glory Cloud. You see, wonderful things happened in our services which we can't understand, but we know it's the Glory. We've had angels show up in some of our services which were seen by 4, 5 and 6 year old little children. There were huge angels around us and angels all over the place. There was one time in a service when the Lord told me, "There's an angel right there."

I asked, "Where?" "Right there."

So instead of me praying for people I said, "Just come up right here. Walk right over there."

When they walked there they just fell out under the power of God. Then I say to the next one, "Walk over there." If the other one hadn't gotten up they would have piled up on top of one another. There was an angel there and anyone who walked past there just fell under God's power.

We need to live in that realm. There are angels to assist us as ministering spirits to work with the heirs of salvation. God wants us to work and expect God's Glory.

Wonderful things happened as we were ministering in the leper colony for several days before Good Friday. Now it's the day before Good Friday and we're leaving the leper colony to go back to Sister Tinyo's house.

❥ Good Friday Miracle ❦

As we're leaving, thousands of people were walking towards us. Sister Tinyo had to keep honking her horn to have them move. The road is filled with people walking and I said, "Where are these people walking?" They're going to a grotto. I said, "They're going to the grotto. What for?" Tomorrow is Good Friday and these are all Catholics. Pretty much everybody in the Philippines is Catholic.

They're going to the grotto and most of them will sleep there tonight because tomorrow is Good Friday. They're doing their rosaries and their novenas and are going to light candles. I said, "How many people go to the grotto tomorrow?" She said, "About a hundred thousand. They come from all over, some from the upper villages and there'll be buses bringing them in tomorrow."

All of a sudden the Holy Spirit said, "Get tracts and give them all a tract." I had five dollars in my pocket and that was it. We're broke. I said, "Sister Tinyo, the Lord said we have to give them all tracts."

She said, "Well I don't know where we are going to get tracts. Oh, wait I know where a Bible bookstore is." I said, "You do?" And she says, "Yeah but it's probably closed by now." I said, "Let's go there."

So we went and we couldn't find anyone. The next morning we went back and it was closed because it was Good Friday. A sign there said We're Closed for the Holiday. She said, "But they live upstairs. " I said, "Really?"

I started throwing rocks to hit the apartment windows on the top floor where they lived. Not real big rocks because I didn't want to break the window but I kept throwing rocks and pretty soon somebody cranked the window open.

"What? What are you ladies doing?" I said, "It's an emergency, come down and open the door. I am from America and I have a word for you from God. Please come down and open the door." They came down and opened the door. I told them that God said we should give tracts to all the people going home from the grotto. Today at 3 o'clock, they will start their trip home from the grotto and I want to have tracts for them.

They talked to each other and said, "We'll see how many tracts we have." They had these nice little booklets, which are 50 cents each in America. They're called *Steps to Heaven and Salvation* with a whole Bible study.

She said, "We have 50,000 of them."

I said, "Great we'll take them all." She said, "They're 50 cents each."

I said, "Well I didn't say I'd pay for them."

She said, "Well that's 25,000 dollars worth of tracts if you bought them." I'm sure the store owners didn't pay that much for them.

I said look, the Lord told me to put these in the hands of the people coming out of the grotto. If you have the tracts and I have the word from the Lord, God will bless you!

They talked together for a while and said, "Okay we are going to give you all 50,000 of them." Now we had a station wagon. When we were through putting these cases into the back of the station wagon we were truly overloaded. Sister Tinyo took me to the road where they would be coming out of the grotto and we drive to a little restaurant. It was a little fruit stand and sandwich type place.

We asked, "Can we put all these cases here?" We stacked the cases all the way up under the little roof so they wouldn't get wet. Sister Tinyo said, "I'm going to run around to the churches because there's no way you and I are going to give out 50,000 of these booklets. When 3 o'clock comes these people will start coming out of the grotto. I'm going to get us help." I said, "While you are getting help I'll just start giving them out."

I saw children in the Philippines run along side buses, jump on the bus and sell their stuff and then jump off. Well I thought I could do that. So I run along one of these big buses and tried to jump on the bus and fell on the ground. When I stood up, another bus was coming toward me taking people home from the grotto. I stop in my tracks and the bus went screech. Don't kill me! I found myself squished between two buses.

As the bus driver came out he said, "What are you doing? Get out of the street!"

When I started to give away tracts it started raining. If you've ever been to the Philippines, when it rains it's not normal rain it's like a gush. I have no time to stop. I have 50,000 of these booklets to give out.

You know when clothes get wet they stick to your body and I have this dress sticking to me and dirt and water are getting all over my sandals. A man came to me and he says, "Lady what are you doing? You're going to get yourself killed." I said, "I'm from America and do you see that building right there? Do you see all those cases? I have from now until 5 o'clock to give out all these booklets because people are coming out of the grotto. They're coming bus after bus."

He said, "You'll never get it done." I said, "My friend has gone to get me help but I don't know where she is. She's been gone already 2 hours." He said, "Well I'll get you help." He rounds up about 30 people. He says, "Okay tell us what you want us to do." I said, "Well okay, will you interpret for me and explain it to them?" He said, "Yes." I said, "Well these are just little books that tell people about Jesus. I am a missionary and I have to get them in everybody's hands because the Bible says you have to go into all the world and preach the Gospel."

They said, "Okay we'll help you put these booklets all over. There is a group of us and we'll get other people to help."

I said, "You'll be working for the Lord so you need to know the Lord Jesus." They said, "What do you mean?" So I shared the plan of salvation and I had them all join hands and pray and accept Jesus. When Sister Tinyo came back she was surprised I had about 30 people all getting on the buses passing out the tracts.

It is very important that you know this. Sister Tinyo's last name is very well known in the Philippines. Her relatives were in the highest positions in the politics of the Philippines. So about the time she arrives where I am the Police Department shows up because we are stopping buses. When we stop one bus it stops 4 or 5 other buses.

We were jamming traffic. By now a hundred thousand people were coming out of the grotto. Sister Tinyo said to the police, bless her heart, my name is such and such Tinyo and my uncle is so and so. We have permission from the highest authority to stop these buses and distribute these booklets. They didn't know we were talking about God – the highest authority. They thought it was from the politics and the highest authority in their country.

All of a sudden, four or five policemen parked their cars and took whistles out. They started stopping all the buses and would fine anybody that went past us. They would stop the buses and say, "Okay jump on and do what you have to do. I'll give you 5 minutes." They stopped and started traffic all day until every one of the 50,000 tracts were given out. By 5 o'clock we are exhausted. In fact we didn't have enough tracts for all of the 100,000 people. God can change a country with one supernatural event. When God speaks to you He will bring it all together. He gave us the tracts. He gave us the laborers. He gave us the highest authority in the land to stop traffic. God even fined those buses who didn't stop.

We serve an awesome God who wants us to walk in the realm of the Supernatural. God wants us to live in that realm because there are so many wonderful things that can happen when we live in the realm of the Supernatural. We saw miracles in the jail, the leper colony, the 50,000 tracts and the 30,000 Bibles which were all given away.

God used every single one of us and He wants to use you too.

CHAPTER 5
Divine Connections

God wants us to have divine connections which happen when we are led by the Holy Spirit.

Romans 8:1

There is therefore now no condemnation to those who are in Christ Jesus, who do not walk according to the flesh, but according to the Spirit.

Romans 8:5-7

For those who live according to the flesh set their minds on the things of the flesh, but those who live according to the Spirit, the things of the Spirit. For to be carnally minded is death, but to be spiritually minded is life and peace. Because the carnal mind is enmity against God; for it is not subject to the law of God, nor indeed can be.

Romans 8:14-17

For as many as are led by the Spirit of God, these are sons of God. For you did not receive the spirit of bondage again to fear, but you received the Spirit of adoption by whom we cry out, "Abba, Father." The Spirit Himself bears witness with our spirit that we are children of

God, and if children, then heirs – heirs of God and joint heirs with Christ, if indeed we suffer with Him, that we may also be glorified together.

God wants us to know that there will be suffering for doing the work of God but the glory is so awesome. God wants us to be led by the Holy Spirit in everything we do.

❧ Our Marriage ❧

In our case, the divine connection brought Marty and me together.

My Pastor had asked me if I could change my ministry schedule in order to work with my home church for a season. If I hadn't been home, I would never have met Marty. He had been in an accident while passing through town and had to stay hospitalized. He had to stay in my area for treatments for a severely broken leg.

God was orchestrating both of our footsteps so we could meet.

Marty's friend Mark had found a flyer about our Healing Meetings. He attended and was filled with the Baptism of the Holy Spirit one night. He was under the power of God on the floor. He heard a voice say to him, "You have to tell Marty. He needs to be in these meetings."

Marty came to the next day's meeting. After that, I invited Marty to an outreach the next Saturday. At

the outreach, Mark was taking photos of all the different witnessing teams. Marty and I had just led a family
to the Lord, when he came to take a photo of us.

Marty put his arm around me, on my shoulder. I am
now under Marty's arm. I hear: "This is where you
belong."

I'm thinking, "Under this guy's arm?"
Mark is trying to take the photo and says, "Get that
funny look off your face, Joan!" Little did he know
what I'd just heard. Then I heard the same words
again. I just shook them off.

I asked Mark and Marty to help take my books and
tapes to my car because I was traveling to Seattle. I
gave each of them one of my testimony tapes as a
thank you for helping me.

While I was preaching in Seattle I was awakened
each night and kept hearing "You are going to marry
this man, Marty." I was confused and called my Pastor
for prayer.

When I got home Mark told me, "Marty needs to
talk to you."

When Marty and I got together he said, "I don't
know how to explain this to you, I've been listening to
your testimony tape the whole time you were gone.

"I don't know what came over me; God dropped
something down deep into my heart from heaven. He
said, 'Protect Joan and take care of her. Help her with
the ministry.'"

Neither one of us was looking to be married or
even wanted to be married, but we both realized God
supernaturally put us together as a couple.

At the time, a few people felt God had not put us together. But we quickly came to realize God had given both of us the same heart. We both are plow horses for God and hard workers. All we cared about, and still care about is advancing God's Kingdom, seeing God's glory be manifested and seeing people saved, healed and filled with the Holy Spirit.

Our heartbeat is to see lives changed for God. We are a powerful team working together on God's behalf.

Over the years, many of those who told us our marriage was not of God, have come to us. They have apologized and said, "Truly, God has put the two of you together!"

AN IMPORTANT NOTE.

Don't go looking to be married. Wait for God to bring you the perfect mate. God orchestrated our marriage and we are madly in love and have been totally blessed.

We pray that you also may have a supernaturally orchestrated marriages.

❥ Fishing Trip ❦

Marty and I were at a week long tent meeting in San Diego, California. It took two days to drive home pulling this great big tent trailer. We're exhausted and we got in quite late. As we were getting closer to home I remember saying, "Wow, we're going to have a couple of days to rest before we go out to do ministry again."

When we got home, we didn't even unpack. We just left the luggage and everything in the truck.

In the morning, when we wake up, Marty said, "We have to go fishing."

I said, "I'm tired. I don't want to go fishing." We live on the Columbia River which is a beautiful huge river with lots of fish.

He said, "But we can't go fishing here."

I said, "What do you mean we can't go fishing here? There's great fish two to three miles from where we are."

Marty says, "No, we have to go to Lewiston, Idaho."

I said, "Honey, that's a hundred miles and we just drove two days to get home. I'm exhausted."

He said, "I really feel that we need to go there."

My husband Marty is very sensitive to the Holy Spirit. So we get into the truck and off we go up to Lewiston. Not everybody knows where this fishing hole is. It's kind of off the road and there are some bushes and stuff there. When we got there Marty goes fishing.

I'm in a lawn chair resting when Marty comes back to where I was and says, "There's a lady over there by the fishing hole that's sitting on a log and she looks pretty bad like she's been beat up. I don't think I should walk up and approach her right now because I might scare her. So, honey, can you go minister to her?"

I walked over to see her and the Lord tells me to sit right on her log even though there are other logs there.

So I sit on her log and she looks at me as if to say, "Why are you sitting on my log?"

As soon as I sat there I see that she's been beat up. She's got stitches all over the place. Her lips are all puffed up. I said, "Honey, God loves you and God has a plan for your life. He's got good things planned for you." She just looked at me and said, "No, He doesn't. I came here to kill myself. I just checked myself out of a hospital and came down to kill myself. How do you know about this place?"

I said, "My husband knows about this place because it's a fishing hole he likes to fish in."

That's why we had to get up and go to Lewiston because the Holy Spirit told Marty. We were at the right place at the right time for her. I started sharing with her about the love of Jesus and she doesn't want to hear it.

Then the Holy Spirit says, "She's hungry so stop talking and take her to lunch." Marty and I took her to lunch. She didn't want to go anywhere fancy because she's all beat up with stitches.

At lunch she started sharing with us that she was a prostitute. She had messed up her life and lost her children. She was with some truck driver up in the mountains doing you know what they do. On her way back she said she heard a voice say that he's going to kill her. So when he down geared the semi, she jumped out.

When she jumped out of the truck, she went over a little cliff and ended up in the hospital. While she was in the hospital she realized that nobody loved her and nobody cared so she decided to go and kill herself.

Well after we ate and went back to sit on the log, I started sharing with her about Jesus. I asked her to pray and accept Jesus. She says, "I will but I don't know if it will work because I don't think Jesus loves me."

She accepted Jesus into her heart. Then I started talking to her about what she wanted. She said, "Peace."

I shared that the peace of God comes from the Holy Spirit. I said "Let's pray for you to receive the Baptism of the Holy Spirit." She started speaking in tongues and the sound just bellowed out of her. Not only was she praying in tongues, she started singing in tongues. The Lord blessed her.

She was transformed. I asked her what she felt. She said, "I feel the peace of God." God touched her and healed her and set her life on course.

I'm so glad I didn't argue with Marty when he said, "Let's go!" Marty was obedient and led by the Holy Spirit.

❧ 9/11 Divine Appointment ❦

As you all know, 9/11 happened several years ago. Just like everybody else we watched it on TV. We had just gotten up and were having coffee and sitting together when he turned the news on. I actually thought Marty was watching some kind of movie.

He said, "Honey, look, this is happening right now." I asked, "What?" He said, "Yeah, right now that airplane just went into the First Tower." Of course everybody's watching that live. Then we watched the plane go into the Second Tower and everybody was in shock.

Everybody started calling me because they know I'm in New York all the time. My phone rang all day long. "Are you in New York? Are you in New York?" I said, "No, I'm not."

The Holy Spirit told me to fly to New York. So, I said to Marty, "Marty, I've got to go to New York." Marty looked at me and said, "No, no, no, honey. You're not going to New York." That's the only time ever in our ministry that Marty said no. He never says no.

It's just that he loves me. He saw what's happening and he wanted to take care of me because he loves me so much. He's a wonderful husband and does protect me.

I said, "God, we have a little bit of a problem. You told me to go to New York and Marty's saying no. I'm not going to argue with Marty. So if You want me to go to New York and minister You have to speak to Marty."

Well anyway, that night Marty had a dream. In the dream, the Lord came to him and said "Do not be afraid. I'm sending your wife to New York and I will have people take care of her. I will line everything up so you do not need to be afraid. Release her to go."

The next day, when I woke up in the morning Marty said, "Honey, the Lord told me I don't need to be afraid. He has everything in control and He would take care of you supernaturally."

It wasn't more than about a half an hour after Marty said that to me that my phone rang. It was a lady I know in New York who lived not too far from where the two towers were.

She said, "The Holy Spirit spoke to me this morning and told me to call you because you were coming to New York and going down to the Twin Towers. You will be ministering to people around the grounds. The Lord told me to call you and tell you to stay at my house. You don't need to worry about a place to stay. Furthermore, I am supposed to take you wherever you need to go."

Within two or three hours our phone rings again. Mary Joe, a lady who works with our ministry said, "The Holy Spirit said you're going to New York. Is that true?" I said, "Yes."

She says, "I'm going with you to help you."

Then Val and Becky, all from different locations called and wanted to go to New York with me. I said, "We already have a place to stay."

Before I flew to New York I called Pastor Leyton Smith. His church was affected by the Twin Towers and they couldn't have church services because of what had happened. They rented a hall in a hotel to have services because the church building was too close to all the ash and the debris.

When I called him I said, "The Holy Spirit told me to come. I know you have a TV show and you have a radio show. I want to know if I can come on your TV show and tell everybody to meet me where you are having your church services, so we can go out on the streets and evangelize."

He just said, "You can. I will."

And I said, "How about on the radio?"

He said, "Yes. You can do that too. You can promote it on TV and radio."

We're all in New York now. As we were getting to the TV station Pastor Leyton called me and said, "Are you at the station, yet?" I said, "We're almost there. We're coming up to the station now."

Pastor Leyton said, "I have a problem. We're not at the studio yet. We're stuck in bumper to bumper traffic and we're not going to make it."

I said, "I'm not ready." He said, "It's an hour and a half show." I said, "Ready or not, I guess here we go." So we run in and they set me in front of the TV cameras. I noticed there are phones all over the place. I told my three assistants who came with me, "Get on the phones and we're going to be live."

I just started preaching. Then all of a sudden I started having words of knowledge. I could see people through the screens. I can see right into their houses. I could look into the TV cameras and see people in their houses and I would say, "Betty-so-and-so, you have on a pink dress or you're in your bathrobe or this or that." I knew everything about them. "This is what's wrong with your back. This is what's going on."

They started calling in. "I'm the Betty she prayed for and I've been healed." They started screaming over the phone that they were miraculously healed. I invited them to come to Pastor Leyton's church. We all left the TV station and went straight to the Friday Night

Service. Pastor Leyton had a speaker that night. We thought the service would be over at 10 pm.

People started coming in and saying, "On the TV, you said you'd pray for us." I started praying for people. Pastor Leyton had to use a banquet room in a hotel in that area. So I prayed for people until three o'clock in the morning.

The people downstairs in the bar had to come upstairs if they had to use the restroom and they passed the open double doors of the room in which we were praying.

Some of the people who came up were half drunk. They saw the power of God was happening and people falling everywhere. They came in and walked up to me and they said, "What's happening? What are you doing? Are you hitting these people? Why are they falling on the floor?"

I said to the people from the bar, "Oh, it's just the presence of God." I put my hands on them all. They went out under the power of God and they were on the floor.

When they got up they went downstairs and told everybody in the bar, "There's activities upstairs in the church service." The next thing I knew it was one o'clock in the morning. People in the bar ended up coming upstairs and I started praying for all of them until three o'clock in the morning. It is glorious when people start getting saved.

Other people just kept coming up for prayer from all over the hotel. Surely it was an outpouring of the Holy Spirit. It was just glorious and we had a miraculous move of God. I ended up praying for people until three in the morning. We had a miraculous move of God.

I've been sharing about our experience at 9/11 and how God supernaturally provided a place for me and the three ladies who traveled with me to stay. It was absolutely wonderful. We gave all the glory to God.

We had been ministering all day from seven in the morning to midnight. We were on TV and on the radio and witnessing everywhere around the Twin Towers while it was still on fire. The police, firemen and iron workers were still pulling bodies out of the ashes. We prayed for the workers; they would just hug us and cry in our arms. We ministered all day long and led people to Christ.

The team and I were exhausted; but when we are weak God is strong.

But what was amazing to me is that because of 9/11 and everything being a total chaos in the area. I pray that it will not take another disaster in this world to bring people close to Jesus.

What amazed us was that right after 9/11 all of the churches were out witnessing. People were showing the love of Jesus.

When I went back again three months later, there were fewer people out there witnessing. I went back again six months later, and it's as if they forgot.

Will it take another catastrophe? Will it take something terrible to have people come back to the Lord or for people to get saved?

I know that for years Marty and I, and many pastors that I've talked with all around the country, have plowed and planted seeds and shared the Gospel.

Sometimes we share and share but don't get to see fruit.

But we know, when there's a disaster or when there's a catastrophe or the United States goes into total chaos, all those seeds that have been planted over the years will come up. The people will come and will remember because the Word of God will not return void without accomplishing what it is set forth to do.

Marty and I believe with all our hearts that we are going to see the greatest revival that the world has ever seen. In fact, we know this will happen because it will be the early rain and the latter rain coming together.

♣ Wall Street, New York ♣

I'm going to share another story. We love to be in New York and we love doing outreaches in New York on Wall Street. I've shared some wonderful stories about what happened on 9/11 but this is another Wall Street miracle that happened. This was actually a couple of years before 9/11. We often take people on missionary trips. Anytime you want to go on a mission trip go to our website and find out more information. TAKE NOTE.

We had 54 people from all over the United States come on this mission trip. We planned several outreaches: a big outreach in Central Park and on Wall Street.

At the Wall Street outreach we had permission to set-up a sound system right on Wall Street. We set it up right across from where the George Washington monument is.

We had 135 people on the street witnessing: our 54 people and a group from *Jews for Jesus*. As I stood there preaching about the heartbeat of God, a strong anointing came in through all of the cross streets up and down Wall Street. All of a sudden everything went into slow motion.

I noticed people were stopping and not moving. Then the Holy Spirit just brought a hush over that whole area. People just stopped. The Holy Spirit was on them.

All of a sudden, when I wanted to do the altar call, I said, "Dear, Jesus come into my heart," trying to get them to pray and accept Jesus."

At that moment the police came over right in front of me, they unplugged the sound. Now I have no sound. I can't finish the altar call because the sound's off.

But thank God that our team knew how to lead people to the Lord. Other people and businessmen started dropping on their knees on the sidewalk. The teams were going over leading them to the Lord. Can you imagine people kneeling on Wall Street accepting Jesus? Only a few on Wall Street received salvation but many heard the Gospel and felt the power of God.

All of a sudden a young girl came over to me. She must have been 16 and she said to me, "My mom wants to talk to you. Here's my mom." I said, "Okay, great, Honey."

Marty was standing beside me. She said, "My mom doesn't speak English, she only speaks French."

I said, "Really?"

She said, "Yes. But we were up on the George Washington Monument across the street and we could hear you. My mom turned to me and said, 'I hear every word that lady is saying in French.' I told my mom, 'Mom, she's not speaking French, she's speaking in English.'

"She said, 'I don't care. I'm hearing her in French.

'She's speaking French. I want to be over there and I want to ask Jesus into my heart.'"

I thought, "Wow, God did all this?"

We're on the corner of Wall Street and the lady from France and her teenage daughter knelt down on the sidewalk by Marty and me. They prayed, "Dear Jesus, come into my heart. Be my Lord. Be my Saviour. I will follow you, love you and serve you all the days of my life." And so they accepted Jesus.

On that Wall Street trip we had so many wonderful encounters. We're on national TV. One day while I was on TV, a mother called me and said, "Thank you, thank you so much, Sister Joan, for leading my little boy to the Lord."

And I said, "Okay, wonderful."

She said, "Thank you for including sign language for him."

I said, "What?"

She said, "My little boy is deaf. I wasn't watching the show. I was in the kitchen cooking.

"My little boy, who is eight-years-old came over and signed to me that he had just prayed the sinners prayer and accepted Jesus with you over the TV screen."

I said to her, "I don't know how to do sign language."

God is so awesome. You see God is a supernatural God and He can do whatever He wants, however He wants to. We just need to live in the Supernatural until it becomes natural.

Later we went to Central Park and worked there with 300 churches. It was amazing. They said, "Joan, we're going to let you do the altar call." It was one o'clock in the afternoon and we only had a permit from Central Park to be there until six. I preached and started the altar call at one o'clock and people were still coming to the altar to get saved at six o'clock. It was such a continual flow of people being saved; I've never seen an altar call last so long.

❧ Lady on a Plane ☙

I'm going to share another story about a lady at an airport. I was busy and I wasn't paying attention. The Holy Spirit soon got my attention. I was in the airport ready to get on the plane and the Holy Spirit says, "Hug that lady." I just grabbed her and I hugged her. As I'm hugging and squeezing her the Holy Spirit has me say to her, "Don't be afraid. Your husband is not going to divorce you. You don't have to be afraid of how to raise your children by yourself because I am working on your husband and he will serve Me and he will not leave you."

She slightly pushed me back a little bit and she says, "Hallelujah, praise you Jesus. Hallelujah, praise you Jesus!"

When I get on the plane she stopped me and she said, "I don't know who you are, lady. But, thank you for being obedient. My parents are pastors and I flew here to spend time with my husband because we've been separated for a little while and he asked me for a divorce. I'm flying back and I've been sitting in the airport worrying. I know now that God is in control."

You know there's no way this can be done in the natural. None of these things can happen in the natural. God wants us to live in a realm of the Supernatural every day whether it's for an elderly adult, or for a child, or for an outreach in a city, or doing a Mission Trip.

So God wants you to walk in the realm of the Supernatural. He wants you to have your own divine appointments, divine encounters where you're led by the Holy Spirit.

❦ Harvest in New York ❦

Just recently we did a big event in Brooklyn, New York. The pastors we worked with ordered a truck loaded with one thousand boxes of pre-boxed groceries. There were 40 pounds of groceries in each of those boxes. Over 2,000 people showed up and several hundred accepted Jesus.

You see, we believe that something's going to happen in the Spirit realm. There's going to be a sovereign move of God and we will see the greatest harvest and the strongest anointing. It won't be just with pastors and ministers. It's going to be where God will use the whole body of Christ. The whole body of Christ will be busy because God has anointed them. You're going to be part of God's outpouring.

That's why it's so crucial that this book, *When the Supernatural Becomes Natural*, gets inside of you. Study it and step out. Start doing those things God tells you to do.

We believe that one on-fire Christian can walk into a mental ward, stand in the middle of that ward and say, "In Jesus' name."

All of a sudden, everybody in that hospital will say, "What? What? What happened? What happened?" All those people won't need to be in a mental hospital anymore.

We believe that saints of God will walk in the Supernatural. They will walk into hospital rooms, start praying for people and the hospitals will empty out. We believe there will be such a move of God that whole cities will be weeping and crying. They will drop to their knees and call out to the Lord their God and accepted Jesus.

CHAPTER 6
White Earth Indian Reservation

I am a Magnet and things come to me. I am highly favored. Money comes to me. Things come to me. I am favored by God because I am a child of God. Because I say it all the time, things come to me.

I was asked to go to the White Earth Native American Reservation. We planned for a year in advance to hold a huge crusade in a football field. We advertised in the White Earth newspaper that we are going to have a football field full of pots, pans, dishes, and everything you can think of to give away.

The Chief Board said, "Okay." They would promote it so they put it in the White Earth paper, on the radio and wherever they could find a place.

When we arrived a year later we had already advertised about doing a big outreach. When I asked the people what did they have? They said just some used clothing. But, I wanted to show the Native Americans that God loves them enough to give them new things.

I arrived Sunday morning and the outreach was the next Saturday. There was nothing to give away but a few used things.

I'm thinking, "God you told me to do this and I have no idea what's going to happen at the outreach."

Sunday night, all of a sudden, after the service some people came to me and said, "Sister Joan can we talk to you?" I said, "Yes." They said, "We saw your show one night about 10 o'clock on nationwide TV. Marty and you gave away groceries, pots, pans, and dishes. We said to each other, 'We need to meet these people. Let's go to California and meet them. Let's set up an appointment.'"

Then the lady's husband said, "Let's do it tomorrow because it is really late. Well the next day we went to your website and to our surprise found out you are here. So we don't have to call California, you are here and preaching in our town here in Minnesota.

"We have a problem which needs your help." I said, "Fine how I can help you?" They said, "We have an entire warehouse of about 30,000 dollars worth of brand new things and we have to have it out of the warehouse before the first of the month. Can we give it to you?"

I exclaimed, "Can you give it to me?" They said, "Yeah, it has to be out before next week. Because you're having this big outreach this Saturday, can we give it to you?" Well not only did they give us those things, they also came and did puppets, skits and brought their sound system.

But let me share with you what God had prepared in advance. We had 30,000 to 40,000 dollars worth of things. The entire football field was filled from one end to the other.

We didn't have junk. We had girl's wool coats that were worth a hundred dollars each. We didn't have only one box, we had 10 or 20 cases, all different sizes. We had tool sets. We had hundreds of comforters from Penny's with the skirting and pillows that matched. We had blankets and clothes and designer jeans. We even had bikes.

The chief came by in the morning before the event and said, "I came by to see what kind of junk you're giving us. You white people! You stole our land!" He was chewing me out and I said, "I didn't do it. I wasn't even born when they took your land. We are trying to bless you."

He said, "Well, let me see what you have." He started walking around looking at all this brand new 'top of the line' stuff. He went to one table and he said, "Oh these are American girl coats."

I said, "Yes, I know." He said, "I tried to buy my daughter one of these but they're a hundred dollars." I said, "You can have one for your daughter. We have 10 boxes over here. What size does she wear?"

"No, I don't want any of your stuff." He said, "I just came to check it out. I'm on my way to my radio station because we have a radio station for the whole reservation and I talk to all my people early every Saturday morning."

I said, "Well, it would really be a shame to take all of these beautiful things and bring them somewhere else because your people didn't come out and get them."

He says, "They'll be here."

On the radio he told them what was there. He said, "Every one of you go get as many things as you can because it is nice and it is new. I'm going to have my people there but I don't want to see any of you going there and getting Jesus. I'm going to have spies there all over the place."

So we couldn't get anybody to come to the altars but that's okay. God knows a way because they were all hearing the gospel even if there were spies there.

A year later, we were doing another big outreach there on *White Earth Reservation*. Their new Chief, Noma is a born again believer.

Blessings of Hope said they'd give us a truck load of groceries to take up to the reservation because we were doing a tent meeting. It was really awesome because we didn't have any transportation to get their groceries from Pennsylvania to Minnesota, so we prayed. We were given the names of some people to call. We were told, "You can't talk to the boss. You have to do it via email."

I made a phone call anyway. People were praying for us because we got right to the owner and I said, "We have no money whatsoever. We have a whole truck load of groceries and we have to get it up here before the tent meeting."

The owner called back and said, "We'll deliver it." So it came 2,100 miles and showed up in time and they didn't charge us anything.

The Native Americans had so much food because God is supernatural and He knows how to do divine connections. He wants to bless us in everything we set our hands to do for Him.

1 Kings 17:8-16

Then the word of the Lord came to him, saying, "Arise, go to Zarephath, which belongs to Sidon, and dwell there. See, I have commanded a widow there to provide for you." So he arose and went to Zarephath. And when he came to the gate of the city, indeed a widow was there gathering sticks. And he called to her and said, "Please bring me a little water in a cup, that I may drink." And as she was going to get it, he called to her and said, "Please bring me a morsel of bread in your hand."

So she said, "As the Lord your God lives, I do not have bread, only a handful of flour in a bin, and a little oil in a jar; and see, I am gathering a couple of sticks that I may go in and prepare it for myself and my son, that we may eat it, and die."

And Elijah said to her, "Do not fear; go and do as you have said, but make me a small cake from it first, and bring it to me; and afterward make some for yourself and your son. For thus says the Lord God of Israel: 'The bin of flour shall not be used up, nor shall the jar of oil run dry, until the day the Lord sends rain on the earth.'"

She went away and did according to the word of Elijah and she and her household ate for many days. The bin of flour was not used up or dried up. The jar of oil remained full according to the word of the Lord spoken by the Prophet.

There's the story where the Lord God sent Elisha to a woman. She had two sons and her husband died.

2 Kings 4:1-7

"Your servant my husband is dead, and you know that your servant feared the Lord. And the creditor is coming to take my two sons to be his slaves."

So Elisha said to her, "What shall I do for you? Tell me, what do you have in the house?" And she said, "Your maidservant has nothing in the house but a jar of oil."

Then he said, "Go, borrow vessels from everywhere, from all your neighbors – empty vessels; do not gather just a few. And when you have come in, you shall shut the door behind you and your sons; then pour it into all those vessels, and set aside the full ones."

So she went from him and shut the door behind her and her sons, who brought the vessels to her; and she poured it out. Now it came to pass, when the vessels were full, that she said to her son, "Bring me another vessel."

And he said to her, "There is not another vessel." So the oil ceased. Then she came and told the man of God. And he said, "Go, sell the oil and pay your debt; and you and your sons live on the rest."

You see God knows how to take care of us and the Bible says, seek ye first the Kingdom of God and His righteousness and all these things will be added unto you. God will take care of you and He'll watch over you.

God wants us to walk in the realm of the Supernatural. He knows how to pay off your bills. He knows how to get you a house. He knows how to get you a car. He knows how to take care of your family. He knows how to make your food supply multiply. So trust the Lord.

❧ Supernatural Prosperity ❧

Psalm 35:27

Let them shout for joy and be glad, who favor my righteous cause; and let them say continually "Let the Lord be magnified, who has plea-sure in the prosperity of His servant."

God wants us blessed.

Psalms 118:25

Save now, I pray, O Lord; O Lord, I pray, send now prosperity.

Psalm 122:6

Pray for the peace of Jerusalem: "May they prosper who love you."

We should pray for Jerusalem because God said when we stand for Jerusalem and pray for Jerusalem you will prosper. Let me tell you how Marty related to a Jewish lady. My husband's so cute. He's so funny and I love him.

We had a trailer we were trying to sell. We had a certain price which we were going to sell it for. A lady agreed to buy it for that price and was about to write out her check.

As we talked with her, we found out she was Jewish. Marty said, "Oh, I didn't know you were

Jewish! Write the check for five hundred dollars less."
I thought why did you do that?

Marty said to me, "She's Jewish and if we bless her because she's Jewish we'll be blessed."

We support many ministries in Israel because we understand that if we support Israel, the homeland of His chosen people, God's Word says we will be blessed.

Matthew 6:33

Seek ye first the kingdom of God and his righteousness all these things will be added unto you.

❧ The Five Hundred Dollar Blessing ❧

Marty and I had just finished a tent revival in southern California. We were headed home to Kennewick, Washington and were on our second day of travel driving the big truck and pulling the trailer behind us.

Marty said to me, "Do we have any more money?"

I said, "No, and all of our credit cards are maxed out."

Marty said, "We have a problem. We don't have enough gas to get home."

I said, "We are totally broke."

Then he took my hand and we prayed for God to provide for us. All of a sudden the phone rang. It was an African pastor who was preaching in London, England. He was calling long distance and he said,

"About an hour ago God told me to Western Union you $500 because you would need it."

He said, "Be blessed."

What a God we serve. He truly knows how to take care of His children.

❧ The Miracle House ❧

Channel of Love Ministries had just bought a house and was starting a half-way house for men. I was in the middle of having a Ministry Board Meeting in my home, when my phone rang.

A realtor said, "Are you still looking for a house?"

I said, "No", and started to hang up when I heard the Holy Spirit say, "Go buy this house."

Then I heard Him say, "Right Now. Go buy it." I was in the middle of a Board Meeting. The Ministry at that time was out of money. How could I buy a house without money?

It's important you know my Mother had just passed away and my inheritance was exactly $9,000.

In obedience to the Holy Spirit I left the meeting and went to look at the house.

It was a huge house on a quarter-acre, with seven bedrooms and a fireplace. It was being remodeled. There was still a little work to be done on it.

I heard the Holy Spirit say, "Buy it Buy it right now"

I was sure the house was high-priced. But in obedience, I told the real estate man, "I will buy this house; how much is it?"

He said, "It is $9000."

I said, "You mean the down-payment?"

He said, "No, the house is in foreclosure. Whoever writes me a check for nine thousand dollars will own it outright."

Immediately, I gave him a $9000 check. Three months later I sold the house and made a great profit. God wants all of us to prosper. He wants all of us to live in the Supernatural.

Just trust in the Lord God with all your heart!

❧ The Prayer Meeting ❧

While I was just starting out in ministry, going to Bible College and still running the franchised corporation, God spoke to me to have an all-night prayer meeting in our workplace every Friday night but not invite anyone. God would bring them by the Holy Spirit. I asked God if I could have someone with me. I did not want to be in the building alone. So I asked an 18-year old Bible student from the Bible College which I was attending at that time. The first night it was just the two of us.

The next week, all of a sudden, people started showing up. Now I don't know how, but people just started coming. The Lord told me not to use the front door of the business but the back door. He said, "Don't lock it and just put a sign on the back door that says, *Don't knock, just come in.*"

It doesn't say prayer meeting it just says, *Don't knock, just come in.* So within two or three weeks we had twenty people praying all night.

Then one night, a lady walked in at about one or two in the morning. She walked in and she stood in the middle of the people walking around her. I walked up to her and said, "Do you want to start praying?"

She said, "Where am I?" I said, "What do you mean?" She said, "I don't understand."

She's looking around really confused. "I left to go kill myself and jump off the bridge. Where am I? How did I get inside this building?"

Well, we did deliverance on her, cast a bunch of devils out of her. She got saved and was filled with the Holy Spirit. By the time the sun came up, she'd been taken out of the kingdom of Satan and into the Kingdom of Jesus. God had ordered her footsteps there.

By the end of four or five months, we had sixty or seventy people praying all night.

They just kept coming and coming. One night there was a pastor who lived thirty miles away from the Tri-Cities. Our building was right by the Sears Building. Our back parking lot was by the front door of the Sears building. The pastor woke up in the middle of the night and the Holy Spirit said to him, "You're going to have Communion in about an hour and a half. So go to your church and get all your communion elements. Make enough for a hundred people and I will tell you where to go." So he goes down to his church and he gets the communion elements.

Then he hears the Holy Spirit say, "Go to the Sears Building in Pasco, Washington." So he drives there and it takes half an hour. He drives to the building and he's in front of the Sears door and across the way is this little light.

It's dark and it's three in the morning. A little light was shining over our door. He looks over and the Holy

Spirit says, "Now turn around and see that little light? Go over there." So he comes over to our back door and it has a sign on it that says, "Don't knock, just come in."

He walks in and there are eighty or ninety people praising God.

He said the anointing just swept him into the building. When we took a little break he said, "I'm here so that we can all have communion." It was just miraculous! You see, we can live in the realm of the Supernatural where God will bring people right to us. God will give you divine connections because He wants us to walk in this realm.

We met for all night Prayer Meetings for almost seven months to a year. Then God told me to change it into Miracle Services and boy did we have Miracle Services. People started coming. We were casting out devils, people got saved, healed and delivered. The place started packing up with people. It was just a revival breaking forth.

CHAPTER 7
From Tent to Tent

Marty and I had just recently gotten married when I had to start going on the road and leave Marty. I went to California because we were still living in Washington State.

We'd talk for hours every day on the phone. He'd always ask me, "How was the service? How many people were saved?" He still does.

I was talking with him before leaving to go to the church and he said, "Honey, I have a wonderful idea and I believe it's from God." I said, "What?"

He says, "We can live in a tent."

I said, "What?"

He says, "Yes. You can come back and get me. We can go to Walmart and buy a tent and everything we need."

I said, "A regular tent like camping?"

And he said,"Yes."

I said, "Marty, I'm going to be in California for three months, preaching all over the state."

He says, "I know, it's summertime."

I said, "I just don't know about this."

He said, "Well, pray about it. When I call you tomorrow morning, let me know what you think."

Well that night, at the service something happened. A young woman about 22 years old came up to me and said, "Sister Joan, would you do a special prayer for me?"

I said, "Sure, I will. What do you want me to pray for you?"

She says, "I want to serve God even if I have to live in a tent."

I thought, "Wow!" I said, "Okay." So I prayed for her.

Well now, I took what was said to me as a sign from heaven that if this young girl wants to serve God even if she has to live in a tent, that was my answer. So I told Marty, we'll do that.

We were going from campsite to campsite. One time we had two days off and we were kicking back at this campsite. In the morning we came out of the tent to get a pot of coffee going. There's this guy with a motorcycle, sleeping on a picnic table in a campsite right beside ours. So we invited him to come over and have coffee with us. Marty's a wonderful cook, so Marty made us all breakfast. We asked our guest, "Well, how is it that you ended up here?"

His name is Dennis and he says, "Well, it's a long story."

We said, "We have all day."

He says, "You see, my dad died about a year and a half ago. Before he died he called me to his bedside, took my hand and said, 'Son, promise me that you will get a house and a car, and that you will prosper and be successful.'

"After my dad died, my quest was to make my dad happy. I got a job and then a second job. Working both jobs, I realized that I hardly saw my wife and my kids. The next thing I know, my wife is having an affair and is filing for divorce and I'm devastated.

"I didn't know what to do. I went to the cemetery where my dad was buried and I said, 'Dad, you've got to release me of this bondage. I can't do it. I'm losing my wife. I'm losing my children because I'm a workaholic.'

"I'm lost and I've got to find something but I don't know what." He lived down by Los Angelus. He continued, "So, I went on a quest. I'm on a quest right now, trying to find something."

I said, "What?"

He said, "I don't know. I'll let you guys know when I find it."

"Well then I took off from LA and drove to San Francisco. I went to the bars, clubs and nightclubs and drove around San Francisco looking for something. But I couldn't find it in San Francisco. So I thought, 'I'll just go a little further. Maybe I'll head up to Portland, Oregon.' So I ended up here in this campground for the night."

Marty and I are looking at each other and grinning because we knew what he was looking for. We start talking and share Jesus with him. That was what he was looking for. After sharing Jesus with him, he received Jesus into his heart. We also started to tell him about the Holy Spirit. We were telling him story after story. All our stories were about the Baptism of the Holy Spirit.

It was late and we said, "Well, Dennis, we're going to call it a night."

Now it's morning and we have to get up and come out of the tent. Instead of Dennis being in his campsite, he's sitting on our picnic table. He says, "I can't wait. I've been waiting. I couldn't sleep. All I thought about was the Holy Ghost all night long.

"So, can I have the Holy Ghost?" We prayed with him and he received the Baptism of the Holy Spirit. He said, "I found it. I found what I've been looking for. I don't need to go to Oregon. I found what I've been looking for. I received Jesus and I received the Holy Ghost."

It was glorious. He went fishing with Marty that day.

The next day we told him, "Now, we're going to church this morning."

He said, "I'll follow you. After church, I'm going back to LA."

So he went with us to the church service. During the whole church service, while the music was going on, tears were running down Dennis' face. When I preached, tears continued running down his face.

He said to the whole church, "I'm going back to get my wife and my children. I found what I was looking for. It was Jesus!"

We had a wonderful experience traveling in that tent.

✦ The Big Tent ✦

I went to the place where I usually prayed early in the morning, "Father in Heaven, we've been faithful to go fishing with the fishing pole. We've been faithful to be fishers of men. We've been faithful to go door-to-door. We've been faithful to do crusades. We've been faithful one-on-one. We've been faithful to tell people about Jesus. But, Lord, give us a net. We're tired of fishing in little ponds. Give us a net." And I started crying and crying.

I went into deep intercession, "God give us souls or we'll die." I was growling in my spirit and I heard the Holy Spirit say to me, "Multitudes, multitudes in the valley of decision for the day of the Lord is near."

The Lord said to my spirit, "You will see more people saved than you could ever imagine." I said, "Thank you, Lord." After an hour or so of this heart-felt prayer, I went home. I had to go to Florida to minister. I spent a little time with Marty. He helped me pack and took me to the airport.

Now, I had prayed that prayer about six in the morning. So when I got to Florida and got to where I was staying, the lady of the house said, "You need to call your husband. He said it's very important. As soon as you walk in call."

I called Marty and he said, "Honey, some people are going to call you at 11:00. And as soon as you get off the phone, call me back."

I said, "What is this all about?"

He said, "No. I'm not telling you what it is about. You have to wait for their phone call."

They called me in Florida and said, "We are business people and we live in San Diego, California. We buy tents for ministries. We had a Board Meeting and were deciding who we're going to bless with tents. So we prayed and we each wrote down the names of those we were supposed to buy the tent for. When we unfolded the papers, we had all written, '*Channel of Love Ministries*, Joan and Marty Pearce.'"

Every single one of them - *Channel of Love Ministries*, Joan and Marty Pearce. On the phone they asked me, "What color tent do you want? What size tent do you want? We will pay for it. All you have to do is go to the tent factory and pick it up."

I don't know why I said it, "I want a tent that sits a 1,000 people. I want it to be red and white to represent the blood of Jesus because He makes you whiter than snow.

"I want the roof on this tent striped red and white. People are going to get healed because by His stripes we were healed."

Three or four months later we swung by and picked up the tent. We had already bought a tent trailer. Marty and I both fasted and prayed and the Lord told us that every Saturday when we do revival meetings and the tent goes up, we are to do an outreach and give away food, clothing, pots, pans and dishes. We've been busy using the tent for the End Time Harvest of souls.

God is faithful and true. So, this is our story *From Tent to Tent*. As we were faithful to be in the little tent, preaching the Gospel while going camping, God saw our faithfulness and we were moved up from the little tent to a huge tent. All for the glory of God and in Jesus' name.

❥ Hollister Tent Meeting ❦

Marty and I did a tent revival meeting in Hollister, California. After the service we all went to a restaurant which was open late and we started talking. Judy, a team member, was with us along with a whole bunch of people and we just started kind of chit chatting with the waitress. Just small talk as she was coming back and forth. Little by little we started talking about Jesus and that we're in town doing a tent meeting.

One of the people on the team said, "You ought to come to our tent meeting and see because we're seeing miracles and people are being healed.

She says, "Oh, I can't come." We ask, "Why?"

She replied, "I'm in jail."

We said, "Well, you don't look like you're in jail."

She said, "I'm on work release but I'm living in the city jail. I only get to come to work. Then the sheriff's department comes and picks me up and brings me back to jail." So Judy was with us and said, "Let me see if I can go down to the courthouse tomorrow and see if you can come to the tent."

The waitress said, "Well I have to be at work at 10." Judy said, "Maybe you could just leave early."

The next day I'm praying and while I'm praying I had a vision. I saw the waitress we met at the restaurant walking into the tent and I say to her, "You want to get saved?" I haven't even talked to her about the Lord. That's all I said and the vision was gone.

Now we're at the tent and the service is over. We've already done altar calls, Baptisms in the Holy Spirit, rededication and prayed for everybody. People are on the floor under the power of God.

I'm getting ready to have somebody do the closing prayer. All of a sudden I see Marty coming from behind the tent signaling like: "Don't stop."

Marty and Judy come in and bring up the lady from the restaurant.

It was like an instant replay of what I saw when I prayed.

Marty brought her up. I looked at her and I said, "You want to get saved."

She said, "Yes I do." I led her to repeat my words: Dear Jesus.

All of a sudden the Holy Spirit hit her, hit Marty, hit another guy on the other side and they all collapsed on the floor. When the waitress hit the floor, she was speaking in tongues. She was only there for a few minutes and was saved and filled with the Holy Spirit.

CHAPTER 8
Divine Protection for Us

Second Timothy 1:7 says, "God has not given us a spirit of fear, but of power and of love and of a sound mind." You see, God wants us to know that He will take care of us.

Acts 5:18-20

And they laid hands on the Apostles and put them in a common prison. But at night, an angel of the Lord opened the prison doors and brought them out and said, "Go stand in the temple and speak to the people all the words of life."

Exodus 14:21-23;27,28

Then Moses stretched out his hand over the sea; and the Lord caused the sea to go back by a strong east wind all that night, and made the sea into dry land, and the waters were divided. So the children of Israel went into the midst of the sea on the dry ground, and the waters were a wall to them on their right hand and on their left. And the Egyptians pursued and went after them into the midst of the sea, all Pharaoh's horses, his chariots, and his horsemen....
And Moses stretched out his hand over the sea; and when the morning appeared, the sea

returned to its full depth, while the Egyptians were fleeing into it. So the Lord overthrew the Egyptians in the midst of the sea. Then the waters returned and covered the chariots, the horsemen, and all the army of Pharaoh that came into the sea after them. Not so much as one of them remained.

The Israelites crossed the Red Sea and after Pharaoh's entire army went in, the water came down on top of them. You know, God was and still is able to do beyond what we can think.

The walls of Jericho also came down supernaturally. Also read in the Old Testament about Gideon's army going into battle. The Lord did it all.

Look at Samson and all he did and his great strength. God did great, great things and God still does great things. He protects us. We do not need to be afraid.

Daniel 3:22-25

Therefore, because the king's command was urgent, and the furnace exceedingly hot, the flame of the fire killed those men who took up Shadrach, Meshach, and Abed-Nego. And these three men, Shadrach, Meshach, and Abed-Nego, fell down bound into the midst of the burning fiery furnace.

Then King Nebuchadnezzar was astonished; and he rose in haste and spoke, saying to his counselors, "Did we not cast three men bound into the midst of the fire?"
They answered and said to the king, "True, O king."
"Look!" he answered, "I see four men loose, walking in the midst of the fire; and they are not hurt, and the form of the fourth is like the Son of God."

You know, if God is willing to go into the fire with us we do not need to be afraid. God wants us to know that He'll take care of us.

❧ Daniel and the Lion's Den ☙

Daniel 6:16-23

So the king gave the command, and they brought Daniel and cast him into the den of lions. But the king spoke, saying to Daniel, "Your God, whom you serve continually, He will deliver you."
Then a stone was brought and laid on the mouth of the den, and the king sealed it with his own signet ring and with the signets of his lords, that the purpose concerning Daniel might not be changed.

Now the king went to his palace and spent the night fasting; and no musicians were brought before him. Also his sleep went from him. Then the king arose very early in the morning and went in haste to the den of lions.

And when he came to the den, he cried out with a lamenting voice to Daniel. The king spoke, saying to Daniel, "Daniel, servant of the living God, has your God, whom you serve continually, been able to deliver you from the lions?" Then Daniel said to the king, "O king, live forever! My God sent His angel and shut the lions' mouths, so that they have not hurt me, because I was found innocent before Him; and also, O king, I have done no wrong before you."

Now the king was exceedingly glad for him, and commanded that they should take Daniel up out of the den. So Daniel was taken up out of the den, and no injury whatever was found on him, because he believed in his God.

❧ God Protects Me ☙

God wants you to know that He will protect you even when things try to hurt you. I'd like to share a few stories of how God has divinely protected me.

Once, I was taking people out on the streets in Seattle. I had about thirty-five young people with me. We were going up and down the street witnessing to the people. There were lots of people on the streets. Some of them were drunk, some of them weren't.

There was one guy who kept harassing the teenagers. I finally told him, "Stop." He was getting very angry with me, so one time he was so angry with me he said, "Lady, I don't like you." He's drunk and he's sharing Scriptures. He was sharing the Scriptures very accurately.

He knew the Scriptures but he's drunk. It was a bad witness. So I said, "Stop this!" I had to come to him three or four times. He said, "I don't like you." He tried to hit me with a beer bottle he threw at me. When he opened his hand to throw it at me, even though his hand was wide open, the beer bottle was stuck to his hand. He tried three times to throw this beer bottle at me. He got beer all over me but the bottle was stuck to his hand. As soon as he pointed it in a different direction, it flew out of his hand and broke.

Later we did deliverance on him. We cast some devils out of him on the streets, and had him rededicate his life to Jesus. Well, the next day, I'm preaching at the church and all the teenagers who were out on the streets with me suddenly looked at me as I'm getting ready to preach. I thought, why are they staring at me so funny? Then the man who tried to hit me with the beer bottle, came walking in.

I am at the pulpit, and he walks in and stands in front of me. The pastor had just given me the mike and the man said, "Can I talk?" I don't know if I should let this man have the mike. I looked at the pastor and he gave me the signal: "It's up to you."

You know, whatever the Holy Spirit tells you to do, you need to do it.

I said, "Okay" and handed the man the mike. He stood there with tears running down his face and spoke to the entire crowd of about three to four hundred people. He said, "I used to be a pastor. A pastor of a large church. I pastored for years. I built the church from scratch. But my wife went off with my associate pastor and the denomination I was in said that because I was divorced, I could not pastor the church anymore.

"So the denomination took the church from me. I was full of anger because I built the church. It wasn't my fault my wife ran off. Because of my anger I started drinking, started to wander the streets and started to mess myself up. When the teenagers were sharing Scriptures and I started sharing Scripture after Scripture, the peace of God came in me. I knew I was drunk, and I knew I was out of order, and I knew I tried to beat up your Evangelist. But I asked God if He will forgive me."

He dropped to his knees with his hands up in the air saying, "God, please. You've called me. I know I've messed up my life but re-establish me. Please." He started praying and rededicating his life. Before I knew it, thirty teenagers came up hugging him and holding him, crying with him and praying with him.

I never did get to preach that day. I asked, "How many of you have unforgiveness toward the people who have hurt you?" The rest of the meeting was spent praying for people to forgive those who hurt them and rejected them. It was a glorious service and it was all supernatural.

❧ Angel Protection ❦

I was preaching in a church in Montana one Sunday morning. After the church service we all went to lunch and a lady said to me, "Sister Joan, will you witness to my husband because he's not saved. He's really mean. Can you come to my husband's house and try to get him saved?"

I said, "Yes."

The pastor said, "You just should have never said that."

I said, "Why?"

He said, "This guy's so terrible he comes to my church services and just sits in the parking lot and blasts the horn all the time. He also has a billboard in his front yard that says don't go to such and such church because it's a cult. He also made flyers and went door to door telling people not to go to my church. He's such a very bad person. He hates me."

I said, "Well, I promised her that I would go."

It was summer so when I knocked on his door, the door opened. It wasn't really shut and there was no screen. He was in his bathrobe and said, "What do you want?"

I said, "I'm a Christian and I'm here to share Jesus."

He said, "Yeah, well, didn't you read that sign out there? Are you from that church? Well, I want nothing to do with God or Jesus. You see this house? Look at it. It is so filthy."

I said, "I can see."

Then he said, "Step in." I stepped in and he said, "Look at these dirty dishes, pots and pans. Where is my wife? At church, church, church. You see she blesses the food and it takes hours."

"So I told Satan, I don't want to go to church. I give my soul to you, Satan."

When he said that the Holy Spirit grabbed me and I just came right in his face. I said, "You don't want to go to hell. Hell is a real place." Then I just preached to him. He listened to me for a few minutes and says, "I don't want to hear anymore of what you have to say." I said, "You need to hear what I have to say." He said, "I don't want to hear it."

The demons swelled up in him. The next thing I know he said, "I don't like you either. I sold my soul to Satan so don't you worry me." He's six foot tall and all of a sudden he backed up, took his fist and swung at me with everything in him. He swung straight at me and hit me in the jaw.

He hit me in the jaw a second time. Then he did it a third time. He tried to do it a fourth time but this time the Holy Spirit had me say, "You try to touch me again, and my angels are going to pick you up and throw you through the wall." Then he told me to leave.

So when I left I felt no pain. Nothing. A few months later he called the church and said, "I've became a terrible person since I sold my soul to Satan. The lady you sent over told me that I shouldn't have done that because the devil will take more and more. You see, I'm doing things now that I hate. I never thought I would ever do those things. Please help me."

So the pastor went and God set this husband free of demons and he received Jesus. He was filled with the Holy Spirit. He went back to every door where he had put a flyer and asked them to forgive him, because this is a good church. He took down his billboard and replaced it with one that said *Jesus Loves You*. He said to the pastor, I don't know what happened when that lady, Joan came. But I slugged her three times in the jaw and I thought my hand was going to break.

Because you see the angels had protected me.

We have divine protection. We have angels on assignment. God can make the walls of Jericho fall down, shut the lion's mouth and take care of the three Hebrew children in the fire, God can take care of us. We don't need to be afraid.

We have divine protection in Christ. We have angels on assignment to take care of us in everything we do. So, know that God loves you.

❧ Our Prayer For You ❧

Marty and my prayer for each and every one of you is that this book has been a blessing to you. As you have read this book, we pray that you would be blessed.

Marty's and my heart is that you will press in with all your heart to be used in the Supernatural. That the Supernatural becomes so natural in you that everywhere you go you will just go from glory to glory, line upon line, precept upon precept.

As you press in and hunger for more and more of God you'll start seeing legs grow out and the dead being raised. You'll be used to witness and pray for the sick and lead many to Jesus. It will become so natural for you.

You will be walking in the Supernatural every day. God bless you. Go, be a world changer.

Matthew 10:7,8

And as you go, preach, saying, "The kingdom of heaven is at hand. Heal the sick, cleanse the lepers, raise the dead, cast out demons. Freely you have received, freely give."

Meditation Scriptures

Meditate on the Scriptures listed below. They will help you walk in the supernatural as you meditate on them and personalize them for yourself.

John 15:16

You did not choose Me, but I chose you and appointed you that you should go and bear fruit, and that your fruit should remain, that whatever you ask the Father in My name He may give you.

John 15:7,8

If you abide in Me, and My words abide in you, you will ask what you desire, and it shall be done for you. By this My Father is glorified, that you bear much fruit; so you will be My disciples.

1 Corinthians 2:2

For I determined not to know anything among you except Jesus Christ and Him crucified.

1 Corinthians 1:30,31

But of Him you are in Christ Jesus, who became for us wisdom from God – and righteousness and sanctification and redemption – that, as it is written, "He who glories, let him glory in the Lord."

Galatians 2:20

I have been crucified with Christ; it is no longer I who live, but Christ lives in me; and the life which I now live in the flesh I live by faith in the Son of God, who loved me and gave Himself for me.

Colossians 3:1,2

If then you were raised with Christ, seek those things which are above, where Christ is, sitting at the right hand of God. Set your mind on things above, not on things on the earth.

Colossians 1:27

To them God willed to make known what are the riches of the glory of this mystery among the Gentiles: which is Christ in you, the hope of glory.

Ephesians 1:3-10

Blessed be the God and Father of our Lord Jesus Christ, who has blessed us with every spiritual blessing in the heavenly places in Christ, just as He chose us in Him before the foundation of the world, that we should be holy and without blame before Him in love, having predestined us to adoption as sons by Jesus Christ to Himself, according to the good pleasure of His will, to the praise of the glory of His grace, by which He made us accepted in the Beloved.

In Him we have redemption through His blood, the forgiveness of sins, according to the riches of His grace which He made to abound toward us in all wisdom and prudence, having made known to us the mystery of His will, according to His good pleasure which He purposed in Himself, that in the dispensation of the fullness of the times He might gather together in one all things in Christ, both which are in heaven and which are on earth – in Him.

Ephesians 2:4-7

But God, who is rich in mercy, because of His great love with which He loved us, even when we were dead in trespasses, made us alive together with Christ (by grace you have been saved), and raised us up together, and made us sit together in the heavenly places in Christ Jesus, that in the ages to come He might show the exceeding riches of His grace in His kindness toward us in Christ Jesus.

Ephesians 3:14-21

For this reason I bow my knees to the Father of our Lord Jesus Christ, from whom the whole family in heaven and earth is named, that He would grant you, according to the riches of His glory, to be strengthened with might through His

Spirit in the inner man, that Christ may dwell in your hearts through faith; that you, being rooted and grounded in love, may be able to comprehend with all the saints what is the width and length and depth and height – to know the love of Christ which passes knowledge; that you may be filled with all the fullness of God.

Now to Him who is able to do exceedingly abundantly above all that we ask or think, according to the power that works in us, to Him be glory in the church by Christ Jesus to all generations, forever and ever. Amen.

Romans 8:35-39

Who shall separate us from the love of Christ? Shall tribulation, or distress, or persecution, or famine, or nakedness, or peril, or sword? As it is written:

"For Your sake we are killed all day long; We are accounted as sheep for the slaughter."

Yet in all these things we are more than conquerors through Him who loved us. For I am persuaded that neither death nor life, nor angels nor principalities nor powers, nor things present nor things to come, nor height nor depth, nor any other created thing, shall be able to separate us from the love of God which is in Christ Jesus our Lord.

Key Soul-Winning

I. Soul-Winning.
Questions to Ask.
1. If you were to die right now, do you know for sure that you would go to heaven?

2. Suppose you died and were standing before God. If He asked you why He should let you into Heaven, what would you say?

3. Could I take a moment to share with you, so that you can be sure what would happen if you were to die?

II. Salvation.
1. Every person must be born again to know God and have everlasting life (John 3:3; John 3: 16).

2. The reason why we must be born again is found in Romans 3:23 (all have sinned).

3. Romans 6:23 - For the wages of sin is death, but the gift of God is eternal life in Christ Jesus our Lord.

4. Being saved or born again is receiving Jesus as your Lord (Master) and committing yourself to follow His Word (Romans 10:9-10).

5. Ask person if they believe that Jesus died for them and that God raised Jesus from the dead. If they believe these two things they can be saved.

6. Ask to take person's hand. Bow your head in prayer. YOU pray. Ask them to pray with you. (They repeat a phrase-by-phrase prayer after you.)

7. Pray this prayer with them:

Jesus, I ask You to come into my life. I confess with my mouth that Jesus is my Lord. I believe in my heart that God has raised Jesus from the dead. I turn my back on sin. I repent of all my sins. I am now a child of God. Thank you Jesus for saving me.

8. Tell them to tell someone else about their salvation experience. "Now tell someone today that you received Jesus as your Savior."

III. Follow-Through

1. "You are now born again, forgiven and on your way to heaven." Show them that they are now the "righteousness of God" in Christ (2 Corinthians 5:17-21). Also share about their need to renew their minds (Romans 12:1-2).

2. Invite them to come to church and start discipling them.

Steps to Baptism in the Holy Spirit

1. The Holy Spirit is the source of a Powerful Life.

a. Acts 1:8. "Power"and abundant strength and ability to be an overcomer and live a victorious life.

b. John 14:26. Comforter and teacher, Who helps you in your everyday life situations.

c. Acts 19:1-2,5-6. Baptism of the Holy Spirit is a separate experience from the work of the Holy Spirit in conversion.

d. Acts 10:44-46. People were filled with the Holy Spirit and spoke in tongues.

2. What happens when you are filled with the Holy Spirit?

Acts 2:4 - And they were all filled with the Holy Spirit, and began to speak with other tongues, as the Spirit gave them utterance.

The Holy Spirit is already here for every born again person. You do not need to wait for Him. Just ask to receive the Holy Spirit.

Acts 2:38-39 - Then Peter said to them, "Repent, and let everyone of you be baptized in the name of Jesus Christ for the remission of sins; and you shall receive the gift of the Holy Spirit.

"For the promise is to you and to your children, and to all who are afar off, as many as the Lord our God will call."

3. Your mind won't understand or gain anything from speaking in tongues. (It will sound useless and foolish.) You are speaking mysteries to God, not to man.

a. 1 Corinthians 14:2 - For he who speaks in a tongue does not speak to men but to God, for no one understands him; however, in the spirit he speaks mysteries.

b. l Corinthians 14:14-15 - For if I pray in a tongue, my spirit prays, but my understanding is unfruitful. What is the conclusion then? I will pray with the spirit, and I will also pray with the understanding. I will sing with the spirit, and I will also sing with the understanding. (Note: Speaking in tongues is an act of your will. God will not force you to do it, or do it for you.)

4. If you ask for the Holy Spirit in faith, you will receive Him.

Luke 11:13 - "If you then, being evil, know how to give good gifts to your children, how much more will your heavenly Father give the Holy Spirit to those who seek Him."

5. Have the person ask for the Holy Spirit (Luke 11:13). Then lead them into a prayer inviting the Holy Spirit to fill them.

6. Pray for them. Let them know that they, as an act of faith, must open their mouth and let the Holy Spirit fill them.

7. Have them pray this prayer:

Father, I am asking you for the gift of the Holy Spirit.

Jesus, baptize me with the Holy Spirit and fire.

Dear Holy Spirit, come into me and fill me.

Boldly speak out in other tongues. Let the Holy Spirit just fill your mouth and use you.

About Channel of Love Ministries

Evangelist Joan Pearce was radically saved in 1977, and shortly afterwards moved to Washington State. There she was greatly inspired and discipled by the daughter and son-in-law of the late Evangelist John G. Lake. God asked Joan to step out and do a home Bible Study, even though she couldn't read.

Joan recognized God's hand was on her, and that He was calling her into ministry. Her heart cry is for souls and to fulfill Luke 4:18-19, to preach the gospel to the poor, heal the brokenhearted, and bring healing and freedom to the hurting and oppressed – "to proclaim the acceptable year of the Lord."

Today Joan continues in full-time ministry, traveling across the United States and overseas. Channel of Love Ministries is doing "God is Taking the City" campaigns, where Joan and her husband Marty are seeing churches come together in unity to evangelize their cities. Joan also does revivals, church meetings, and city-wide crusades where thousands come to Jesus. Part of her ministry is to teach practical evangelism classes and to conduct Holy Spirit Miracle Services where there are many notable and creative miracles. She and Marty have a heart to feed and clothe the needy and have ministered to the poor throughout the world.

Joan is on TV across the United States, and is on the internet world wide. The Channel of Love Ministries website is **www.joanpearce.org**. She and Marty are fulfilling God's great commission to "Go into all the world and preach the gospel" (Mark 16:15.)

Contacting Channel of Love Ministries

www.joanpearce.org

➤ To write us a note, praise report or prayer request

➤ To see our TV show, *Now is the Time for Miracles*

➤ Learn more about our ministry and its goals

➤ Receive more details about God is Taking the City

➤ Offer financial and practical support

➤ See our current schedule
  Come to our Schools of Ministry

➤ Learn about opportunities to participate in Channel of
  Love Ministries trips

➤ Get information on scheduling meetings for your
  church or group

➤ Order books, CD's and DVD's

➤ Sign up for our free Newsletter

➤ Download our free ministry helps

➤ ... and much more

We look forward to hearing from you!

Channel of Love Ministries Intl.
*Helping you to grow spiritually and
share your faith more effectively!*

Yes, YOU can hear GOD too!
Order No. 0007-B
Price $15.00

Every believer has the right to hear from Heaven. This down to
earth book will challenge you to hear from God!

Let's Go Fishing!
Order No. 0042-B
Price $15.00

Are you wondering? "What's God's purpose and plan for my
life?" "How do I: Draw my loved ones and others to the Lord .... Answer their
questions .... Help my church or group reach out to the lost and needy?" This book
answers your questions.

Now's the Time Bible Studies
Order No. 0043-B
Price $10.00

Here are precious keys for unlocking and releasing God-given
provision, power and authority into your life, and experiencing the precious love
of Jesus. You'll grow spiritually – and be able to share what you've learned with
others.

The Empty Spot
Order No. 0045-B
Price per pkg. of 10 $12.00

An excellent booklet for getting people saved and for discipling
those who have recently received Jesus. This book has led thousands to Jesus. It's
a great witnessing tool!